Presented To

_____

By

_____

_____

Date

_____

THE TREASURY
of
CHRISTIAN CLASSICS
for
CHILDREN

Compiled and adapted by
Rhonda S. Hogan and Mary Hollingsworth

FRONTPORCH
BOOKS

THE TREASURY OF
CHRISTIAN CLASSICS FOR CHILDREN

Copyright © 1999 by FrontPorch Books, a division of Garborg's, LLC
Published by Garborg's, LLC
P. O. Box 20132, Bloomington, MN 55420

ISBN 1-58375-475-X

Illustrated by Roger Lundquist and Larry Ruppert
as represented by Spectrum Studios
Design by Lecy Design

All Bible verses used are from *The Adventures in Odyssey Bible*,
Bible text from *The International Children's Bible*,
New Century Version, copyright © 1986, 1988, 1994
by Word Publishing. All rights reserved. Used by permission.

Compiled and adapted by Rhonda S. Hogan and Mary Hollingsworth
Shady Oaks Studio, 1507 Shirley Way, Bedford, TX 76022

Printed in the United States of America.

CONTENTS

CONTENTS

You tell whatever story that must be told.
And when it's too hard for adults,
you tell it for children.

Madeleine L'Engle

Dear Parents,

"The story's the thing!" For it's the delightful stories of interesting people and exciting events that carry us along through life. It's the stories of youth that stick to our minds like peanut butter sticks to the roof of our mouths. They entertain us, they intrigue us, they influence us, they shape us.

Who can forget the ugly duckling's surprise when he turned into a glorious swan? And how many times as a teenager did you glance into a mirror, thinking *That's me!*

Who can resist the delight of really seeing nature for the first time? Turning sea shells over and over again, like the little girl in *How Margery Wondered*, we marveled at how they were made. Or we sat watching the shoreline for hours wondering who was pushing the waves and where they were coming from.

And who can keep from sniffling a little when we think of the sacrificial love we were taught by the husband and wife in *The Gift of the Magi?* It's a lesson that soaks into our hearts for life.

Classic stories teach classic morals and lessons—lessons like honesty, fairness, sharing, and caring. They give us hope, emphasize humility, and build healthy esteem. They add knowledge, adventure, and emotion to the lives of readers. And best of all, they reiterate the teachings of God and the Bible.

The Treasury of Christian Classics for Children is a collection of wonderful stories that will do these things for today's children. Some are long; some are short. Some are poems; some are stories. Some are well known; some are lesser known. But all of them are good, wholesome stories that reflect strong morals and lessons that children will never forget. Besides, they're just plain fun!

So, settle down in your favorite easy chair with your children all around for an adventure into the classics—the same kind of adventure you had as a child.

The Publisher

THE LION AND THE MOUSE

AN ÆSOP'S FABLE

One day a great lion lay asleep in the sunshine. A little mouse ran across his paw and woke him up. The great lion was just going to eat him when the little mouse cried, "Oh, please let me go, sir, some day I may be able to help you."

The lion laughed at the thought that the little mouse could be of any use to him. But he was a good-natured lion, and he set the mouse free.

Not long after, the lion was caught in a net that had been set by some hunters. He tugged and pulled with all his might, but the ropes were too strong. Then he roared loudly. The little mouse heard him, and ran to where the lion was caught in the ropes.

"Be still, dear lion, and I will set you free, I will gnaw the ropes." With his sharp teeth the mouse cut the ropes, and the lion came out of the net.

"You laughed at me once," said the mouse. "You thought I was too little to do you a good turn. But see, you owe your life to a poor little mouse."

"Mouse," said the lion, "I did not believe that someone so small could ever rescue me, but now I know you are a true friend."

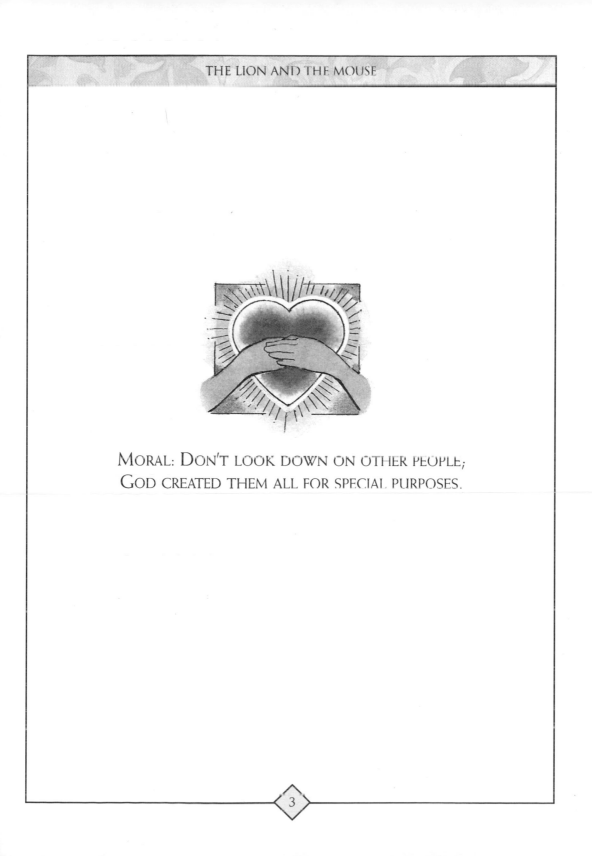

MORAL: DON'T LOOK DOWN ON OTHER PEOPLE;
GOD CREATED THEM ALL FOR SPECIAL PURPOSES.

THE UGLY DUCKLING

HANS CHRISTIAN ANDERSEN

It was lovely summer weather in the country, and the golden corn, the green oats, and the haystacks piled up in the meadows looked beautiful. The stork walking about on his long red legs chattered in the Egyptian language, which he had learned from his mother. Large forests surrounded the cornfields and meadows, and in the middle were deep pools.

It was delightful to walk about in the country. In a sunny spot stood a pleasant old farmhouse close by a deep river, and from the house down to the waterside grew great burdock leaves, so high that under the tallest of them a little child could stand upright. The spot was as wild as the center of a thick wood.

In this snug retreat sat a duck on her nest, watching for her young brood to hatch; she was beginning to get tired of her task, for the little ones were a long time coming out of their shells, and she seldom had any visitors. The other ducks liked much better to swim about in the river than to climb the slippery banks and sit under a burdock leaf to have a gossip with her. At last one shell cracked, and then another, and from each egg came a living creature that lifted its head and cried, "Peep, peep."

"Quack, quack," said the mother, and then they all quacked as well as they could. And they looked about them on every side at the large green leaves. Their mother allowed them to look as much as they liked, because green is good for the eyes.

"How large the world is," said the young ducks when they found how much more room they now had than while they were inside the eggshell.

"Do you imagine this is the whole world?" asked the mother. "Wait till you have seen the garden; it stretches far beyond that to the parson's field. But I have never ventured to such a distance. Are you all out?" she continued, rising; "No, I declare, the largest egg lies there still. I wonder how long this is to last, I am quite tired of it;" and she seated herself again on the nest.

"Well, how are you getting on?" asked an old duck, who paid her a visit.

"One egg is not hatched yet," said the duck, "it will not break. But just look at all the others, are they not the prettiest little ducklings you ever saw? They are the image of their father, who is so unkind, he never comes to see."

"Let me see the egg that will not break," said the duck; "I have no doubt it is a turkey's egg. I was persuaded to hatch some once, and after all my care and trouble with the young ones, they were afraid of the water. I quacked and clucked, but all to no purpose. I could not get them to venture in. Let me look at the egg. Yes, that is a turkey's egg; take my advice, leave it where it is and teach the other children to swim."

"I think I will sit on it a little while longer," said the duck; "as I have sat so long already, a few days will be nothing."

"Please yourself," said the old duck, and she went away.

At last the large egg broke, and a young one came out crying, "Peep, peep." It was very large and ugly. The duck stared at it and exclaimed, "It is very large and not at all like the others. I wonder if it really is a turkey. We shall soon find it out when we go to the water. It must go in, if I have to push it myself."

On the next day
the weather was
delightful, and the
sun shone brightly on
the green burdock
leaves. So the mother
duck took her young
brood down to the
water and jumped in
with a splash. "Quack,
quack," cried she, and
one after another the
little ducklings

jumped in. The water closed over their heads, but they came
up again in an instant. And they swam about quite prettily with
their legs paddling under them as easily as possible. The ugly
duckling was also in the water swimming with them.

"Oh," said the mother, "that is not a turkey; how well he uses
his legs, and how upright he holds himself! He is my own
child, and he is not so very ugly after all if you look at him
properly. Quack, quack! come with me now. I will take you
into grand society, and introduce you to the farmyard. But you
must keep close to me, or you may be trodden upon. And,
above all, beware of the cat."

When they reached the farmyard, there was a great
disturbance. Two families were fighting for an eel's head,

which, after all, was carried off by the cat.

"See, children, that is the way of the world," said the mother duck, wetting her beak, for she would have liked the eel's head herself. "Come, now, use your legs, and let me see how well you can behave. You must bow your heads prettily to that old duck yonder. She is the highest born of them all and has Spanish blood; therefore, she is well off. Don't you see she has a red flag tied to her leg, which is something very grand, and a great honor for a duck. It shows that every one is anxious not to lose her, as she can be recognized both by man and beast. Come, now, don't turn your toes. A well-bred duckling spreads his feet wide apart, just like his father and mother, in this way. Now bend your neck and say 'quack.' "

The ducklings did as they were told, but the other ducks stared, and said, "Look, here comes another brood, as if there were not enough of us already! And what a strange looking object one of them is. We don't want him here." And then one flew out and bit him in the neck.

"Let him alone," said the mother; "he is not doing any harm."

"Yes, but he is so big and ugly," said the spiteful duck," and therefore he must be turned out."

"The others are very pretty children," said the old duck with the rag on her leg, "all but that one; I wish his mother could improve him a little."

"That is impossible, your grace," replied the mother; "he is not pretty; but he has a very good disposition. And he swims as well, or even better, than the others. I think he will grow up pretty. And perhaps be smaller. He has remained too long in the egg, and therefore his figure is not properly formed." And then she stroked his neck and smoothed the feathers, saying, "It is a drake, and therefore not of so much consequence. I think he will grow up strong and able to take care of himself."

"The other ducklings are graceful enough," said the old duck. "Now make yourself at home, and if you can find an eel's head, you can bring it to me."

And so they made themselves comfortable. But the poor duckling, who had crept out of his shell last of all and looked so ugly, was bitten and pushed and made fun of, not only by the ducks, but also by all the chickens.

"He is too big," they all said. The turkey cock, who had been born into the world with spurs and fancied himself really an emperor, puffed himself out. He flew at the duckling. The poor little duck did not know where to go and was quite miserable, because he was so ugly and laughed at by the whole farmyard. So it went on from day to day and it got worse and worse. The poor duckling was driven about by every one. Even his brothers and sisters were unkind to him, and would say, "You ugly creature, I wish the cat would get you." And his mother said she wished he had never been born. The ducks pecked him, the chickens beat him, and the girl who fed the chickens kicked him with her feet. So at last he ran away, frightening the little birds in the hedge as he flew over them.

"They are afraid of me because I am ugly," he said. So he closed his eyes and flew still farther until he came out on a large pond inhabited by wild ducks. There he remained the whole night, feeling very tired and sad.

In the morning, when the wild ducks rose in the air, they stared at their new friend. "What sort of a duck are you?" they all said, coming round him.

He bowed to them and was as polite as he could be, but he did not reply to their question. "You are very ugly," said the wild ducks, "but that will not matter if you do not want to marry one of our family."

Poor thing! He had no thoughts of marriage; all he wanted was permission to lie among the plants and drink some of the water on the pond. After he had been on the pond two days, there came two wild geese, or rather goslings. They had not been out of the egg long, and were very saucy. "Listen, friend," said one of them to the duckling, "you are so ugly, that we like you very well. Will you go with us and become a bird of passage? Not far from here is another pond, in which there are some pretty wild geese, all unmarried. It is a chance for you to get a wife; you may be lucky, ugly as you are."

"Pop, pop," sounded in the air, and the two wild geese fell dead among the bushes, and the water was tinged with blood. "Pop, pop," echoed far and wide in the distance, and whole flocks of wild geese rose up from the bushes. The sound continued from every direction, for the sportsmen surrounded the pond. Some were even seated on branches of trees, overlooking the bushes. The blue smoke from the guns rose like clouds over the dark trees. As it floated away across the water, a number of sporting dogs bounded in among the rushes, which bent beneath them wherever they went. How they terrified the poor duckling! He turned away his head to hide it under his wing, and at the same moment a large terrible dog passed quite near him. His jaws were open, his tongue hung from his mouth, and his eyes glared fearfully. He thrust his nose close to the duckling, showing his sharp teeth, and then,

"splash, splash," he went into the water without touching him.

"Oh," sighed the duckling, "how thankful I am for being so ugly; even a dog will not bite me." And so he lay quite still, while gun after gun was fired over him. It was late in the day before all became quiet, but even then the poor ugly duckling did not dare to move. He waited quietly for several hours. Then, after looking carefully around him, he flew away from the pond as fast as he could. He flew over field and meadow

till a storm arose, and he could hardly struggle against it.
Towards evening, he reached a poor little cottage that seemed
ready to fall and only remained standing because it could not
decide on which side to fall first. The storm was so bad that
the duckling could go no farther. He sat down by the cottage,
and then he noticed that the door was not quite closed. There
was a narrow opening near the bottom large enough for him to
slip through, which he did very quietly, and got shelter for the
night.

A woman, a tomcat, and a hen lived in this cottage. The
tomcat, whom the woman called, "My little son," was a great
favorite. He could raise his
back, and purr, and even
throw out sparks from
his fur if it were
stroked the wrong
way. The hen had
very short legs, so
she was called
"Chickie short legs."
She laid good eggs,
and the woman loved
her as if she had been
her own child. In the
morning, the strange
visitor was discovered,

and the tomcat began to purr, and the hen to cluck.

"What is that noise about?" said the old woman, looking around the room. But her sight was not very good; therefore, when she saw the duckling she thought it must be a fat duck that had strayed from home. "Oh what a prize!" she exclaimed, "I hope it is not a drake, for then I shall have some duck's eggs. I must wait and see."

So the duckling was allowed to remain for three weeks, but there were no eggs. Now the tomcat was the master of the house, and the hen was mistress. They always said, "We and the world," for they believed themselves to be half the world, and the better half too. The duckling thought that others might hold a different opinion on the subject, but the hen would not listen to such doubts.

"Can you lay eggs?" she asked.

"No."

"Then have the goodness to hold your tongue."

"Can you raise your back, or purr, or throw out sparks?" said the tomcat.

"No."

"Then you have no right to express an opinion when sensible people are speaking."

So the duckling sat in a corner, feeling very sad, until the sunshine and the fresh air came into the room through the open door. Then he began to feel such a great longing for a swim on the water, that he could not help telling the hen.

"What an absurd idea," said the hen. "You have nothing else to do, so you have foolish dreams. If you could purr or lay eggs, they would pass away."

"But it is so delightful to swim about on the water," said the duckling.

"It's so refreshing to feel it close over your head while you dive down to the bottom."

"Delightful, indeed!" said the hen. "Why you must be crazy! Ask the cat. He is the cleverest animal I know. Ask him how he would like to swim about on the water, or to dive under it, for I will not speak of my own opinion. Ask the old woman, there is no one in the world more clever than she is. Do you think she would like to swim or to let the water close over her head?"

"You don't understand me," said the duckling.

"We don't understand you? Who can understand you, I wonder? Do you consider yourself more clever than the cat, or the old woman? I will say nothing of myself. Don't imagine such nonsense, child, and thank your good fortune that you have been received here. Are you not in a warm room and in a society from which you may learn something? But you are a chatterer, and your company is not very agreeable. Believe me, I speak only for your own good. I may tell you unpleasant truths, but that is a proof of my friendship. I advise you, therefore, to lay eggs, and learn to purr as quickly as possible."

"I believe I must go out into the world again," said the duckling.

"Yes, do," said the hen.

So the duckling left the cottage and soon found water on which it could swim and dive. But was avoided by all other animals, because of its ugly appearance.

Autumn came, and the leaves in the forest turned to orange and gold. Then, as winter approached, the wind caught them as they fell and whirled them in the cold air. The clouds, heavy with hail and snowflakes, hung low in the sky, and the raven stood on the ferns crying, "Croak, croak." It made one shiver with cold to look at him. All this was very sad for the poor little duckling. One evening, just as the sun set amid radiant clouds, there came a large flock of beautiful birds out of the bushes. The duckling had never seen any like them before. They were swans, and they curved their graceful necks, while their soft plumage shown with dazzling whiteness. They uttered a cry as they spread their glorious wings and flew away from those cold regions to warmer countries across the sea.

As they climbed higher and higher in the air, the ugly little duckling felt quite a strange sensation as he watched them. He whirled himself in the water like a wheel, stretched out his neck towards them, and uttered a cry so strange that it frightened himself. Could he ever forget those beautiful, happy birds? When at last they were out of his sight, he dived under the water and rose again almost beside himself with excitement. He didn't know the names of these birds or where they had flown, but he felt towards them as he had never felt for any other bird in the world. He was not envious of these beautiful creatures but wished to be as lovely as they. Poor ugly creature, how gladly he would have lived even with the ducks had they only given him encouragement.

The winter grew colder and colder; he had to swim about on the water to keep it from freezing, but every night the space on which he swam became smaller and smaller. Finally it froze so hard that the ice in the water crackled as he moved. The duckling had to paddle with his legs as well as he could to keep the space from closing up. He became exhausted at last and lay still and helpless, frozen fast in the ice.

Early in the morning, a peasant, who was passing by, saw what had happened. He broke the ice in pieces with his wooden shoe and carried the duckling home to his wife. The warmth revived the poor little creature. But when the children wanted to play with him, the duckling thought they would do him some harm. So he started up in terror, fluttered into the milk-pan, and splashed the milk about the room. Then the woman clapped her hands, which frightened him still more. He flew first into the butter-cask, then into the meal-tub, and out again. What a condition he was in! The woman screamed and struck at him with the tongs. The children laughed and screamed and tumbled over each other in their efforts to catch him; but luckily he escaped. The door stood open, so the poor creature could just manage to slip out among the bushes and lie down quite exhausted in the new fallen snow.

When winter had passed, the ugly duckling found himself lying one morning beside a pond among the rushes. He felt the warm sun shining and heard the lark singing. He saw that all around was beautiful spring. Then the young bird felt that his wings were strong, as he flapped them against his sides and rose high into the air. They bore him onwards until he found himself in a large garden, before he well knew how it had happened. The apple trees were in full blossom, and the fragrant elder trees bent their long green branches down to the stream that wound around a smooth lawn. Everything looked beautiful in the freshness of early spring. From a thicket close by came three beautiful white swans, rustling their feathers and swimming lightly over the smooth water. The duckling remembered the lovely birds and felt more strangely unhappy than ever.

"I will fly to those royal birds," he exclaimed. "They will kill me because I am so ugly and dare to approach them. But it does not matter, it is better be killed by them than pecked by the ducks, beaten by the hens, pushed about by the girl who feeds the chickens, or starved in the winter."

Then he flew to the water and swam towards the beautiful swans. The moment they saw the stranger, they rushed to meet him with outstretched wings.

"Kill me," said the ugly duckling, and he bent his head down to the surface of the water and waited for death.

But what did he see in the clear stream below? His own image! He was no longer a dark, gray bird, ugly and disagreeable to look at, but a graceful and beautiful swan. To be born in a duck's nest in a farmyard is of no consequence to a bird, if it is hatched from a swan's egg. He now felt glad at having suffered sorrow and trouble, because it enabled him to enjoy so much better all the pleasure and happiness around him. The great swans swam around the new bird and stroked his neck with their beaks as a welcome.

Into the garden presently came some little children, and they threw bread and cake into the water.

"See," cried the youngest, "there is a new one." And the rest were delighted and ran to their father and mother, dancing and clapping their hands, and shouting joyously, "Another swan has come! A new one has arrived."

Then they threw more bread and cake into the water and said, "The new one is the most beautiful of all; he is so young and pretty." And the old swans bowed their heads before him.

Then he felt quite ashamed and hid his head under his wing, because he did not know what to do. He was so happy but not at all proud. He had been persecuted and despised for his ugliness, and now he heard them say he was the most beautiful of all the birds. Even the elder tree bent down its branches into the water before him, and the sun shone warm and bright. Then he rustled his feathers, curved his slender neck, and cried joyfully from the depths of his heart, "I never dreamed of such happiness as this while I was an ugly duckling."

GOD DOES NOT SEE THE SAME WAY PEOPLE SEE.
PEOPLE LOOK AT THE OUTSIDE OF A PERSON,
BUT THE LORD LOOKS AT THE HEART.
1 SAMUEL 16:7

MY SHADOW

BY ROBERT LOUIS STEVENSON

I have a little shadow
That goes in and out with me,
And what can be the use of him
Is more than I can see.
He is very, very like me
From the heels up to the head;
And I see him jump before me
When I jump into my bed.
The funniest thing about him
Is the way he likes to grow—
Not at all like proper children,
Which is always very slow;

For he sometimes shoots up taller
Like an India-rubber ball,
And he sometimes gets so little
That there's none of him at all.
He hasn't got a notion
Of how children ought to play,
And can only make a fool of me
In every sort of way.
He stays so close beside me,
He's a coward you can see;
I'd think shame to stick to nursie
As that shadow sticks to me!
One morning, very early,
Before the sun was up,
I rose and found the shining dew
On every buttercup;
But my lazy little shadow
Like an arrant sleepy-head,
Had stayed at home behind me
And was fast asleep in bed.

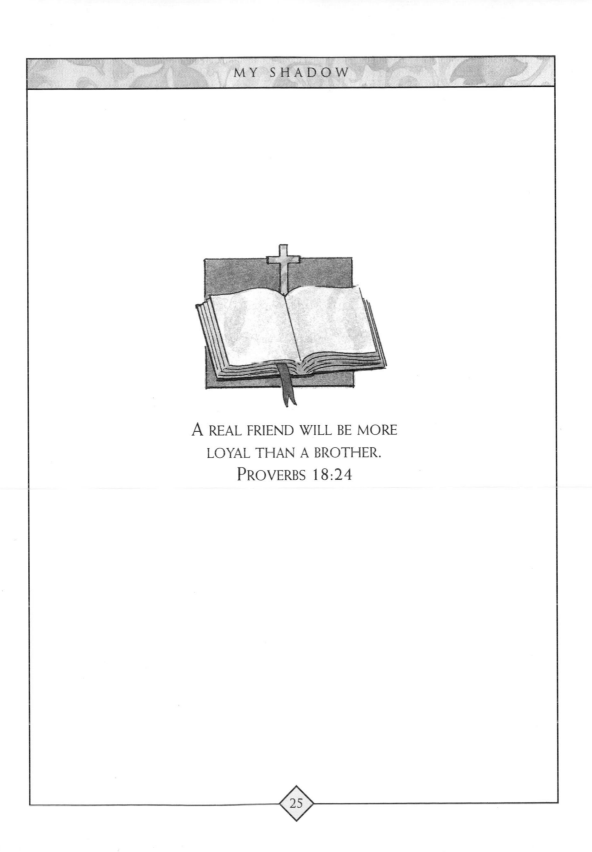

A REAL FRIEND WILL BE MORE
LOYAL THAN A BROTHER.
PROVERBS 18:24

THE LITTLE WHITE BED THAT RAN AWAY

BY PATTEN BEARD

Once upon a time there was a little boy who didn't like to go to bed. When it came time to say good night and go upstairs, he wanted to stay where the fire crackled in the fireplace and where the light was on. He wanted to stay with Mother and Daddy and Jim

Teddy-Bear. He wanted to look at books and play games.

"I don't want to go to bed at all," he said, and he said it very loudly. "I don't like my bed," he added, and he added it very loudly. "I wish I didn't have a bed!" he howled, and he howled it very loudly.

Oh, dear! Upstairs in the little boy's bedroom the Little White Bed heard what he said. It was waiting all warm and cozy, with its blanket turned back to welcome the little boy. Its pillow was all full of dream stories it was going to tell the little boy when he dropped off to sleep.

When the little boy howled what he did, the Little White Bed heard and felt very badly. It decided to run away.

Little White Bed rolled out of its corner and out the door of the little boy's room. It rolled down the hall until it came to the stairs. The Little White Bed started down the stairway. Plumb-bumpety-bump-bump-bump.

Down the stairs went Little White Bed, plumb-bumpety-bump-bump-bump. It rolled across the front hall, squeak-creak. And it rolled out the front door! The Little White Bed was gone.

The little boy looked at Mother. Mother looked unhappy. The little boy looked at Daddy. Daddy looked unhappy, too.

"Well, little boy," they said, "you will have no Little White Bed to sleep in tonight."

Well, the little boy was happy. He felt glad!

He looked at books and played with Jim Teddy-Bear. He was going to play a game when Daddy yawned and got up from his big, comfortable chair and said, "Little Boy, good night. It is late and we must go to bed. Of course, you won't mind if we turn off the light." Then Daddy and Mother went upstairs and left the little boy sitting beside the fireplace, for he had no Little White Bed anymore.

After they had gone to bed, the little boy began to feel sleepy all of a sudden—very tired and very sleepy. The little boy's head went down upon the rug by the fire. It was warm there on the rug, so the little boy didn't mind as much as he might have if it had been cold. Soon he was fast asleep.

After he had been asleep for some time, he woke up suddenly. The fire had gone out, and it was cold. The little boy's arms and legs were stiff and cold. He wanted a pillow for his head, but there was no Little White Bed he could curl up into and be snug. There was no warm blanket. There was no soft mattress. Little White Bed had run away and taken everything with it.

The little boy got up off the rug and walked slowly upstairs in the dark to his room. There was a big empty space where Little White Bed used to be. Now there was no Little White Bed and nowhere to go to sleep except on the floor.

So the little boy said, "I wish my Little White Bed had not run away. I wish I had not said what I did. I wish my Little

White Bed would come back and take me in its lap and let me put my head on its pillow and go to sleep nice and cozy and warm. I wish I had my nice Little White Bed."

He put on his red bathrobe and took a rug and tried to go to sleep on the floor. But every little while he had to jump up and look out of the window to see if he could see his Little White Bed out there in the street. He thought, maybe, he could call to it and tell it he was sorry and perhaps then it might come back.

But when he had gone back to the rug on the floor, he thought he heard a noise at the front door. His heart went pitapat and he listened. Oh, the little boy hoped it might be Little White Bed coming home!

The front door opened, and in walked Little White Bed, creak-squeak-creak! Little White Bed rolled across the front hall. It came up the hall stairs thump-bumpety-bump-bumpety-bump and into the little boy's room. It went right into the corner where it had always stood. It turned back its nice warm blanket for the little boy. In a jiffy the little boy's head was upon the soft pillow. He was warm and comfortable and happy. Before long he was fast asleep, dreaming of the fairy stories that Little White Bed's pillow told him.

Oh, after this, the little boy always went to bed as soon as the clock struck eight. He kissed Mother, and he kissed Daddy, and he said good night to Jim Teddy-Bear right away. He went right upstairs to his Little White Bed as fast as he could go whenever sleep-time came around, and he never wanted to sit up all night long again.

The little boy learned always to be thankful for what he had.

QUEEN ESTHER SAVES GOD'S PEOPLE

THE BOOK OF ESTHER

King Xerxes gave a huge banquet for all the important people in the whole Persian Empire. The banquet lasted one hundred and eighty days! During the party Xerxes showed off all the wealth of his kingdom and the splendor of his own kingship.

One of the things he wanted to show off was his queen. So he sent for Queen Vashti to come to the banquet wearing her royal crown. But she would not go. This made Xerxes angry; so he took Vashti off the throne, and she was no longer queen.

Then all the pretty young women from all over Persia were brought to Xerxes so that he could choose a new queen. He finally chose a beautiful young Jewish girl named Esther. And the king loved her very much.

An important man named Haman hated the Jewish people,. that was because Esther's uncle Mordecai would not bow down to Haman as he passed him on the street. So Haman tricked Xerxes into signing a law saying the Persians could kill all the Jews in the Persian Empire on a certain day. (Haman didn't know that Queen Esther was Mordecai's niece and a Jew.)

When Mordecai heard about the law, he sent a message to Esther, telling her to talk to King Xerxes and save the Jews. But the king had a law that no one was allowed to talk to him unless he called for them—not even the queen. Anyone who disobeyed this law could be killed.

Queen Esther was very brave. So she went to see the king anyway. She said, "If I die, then I die."

But because he loved her, Xerxes did not kill her. Instead, he offered to give her anything she wanted, up to half his whole kingdom! When Esther told him about Haman's plot to kill her people, Xerxes became very angry. So he made another law that said the Jews could fight back if the Persians attacked them. Then he had Haman hanged on the very gallows Haman had built for Esther's uncle Mordecai.

Brave Queen Esther had saved God's people from being destroyed. And every year after that, even up to today, the Jews have remembered the brave thing she did and how God rescued them by celebrating that day with a feast. It was a great day for the people of God.

CHANGEABLE ARTHUR

BY PERCY K. FITZHUGH

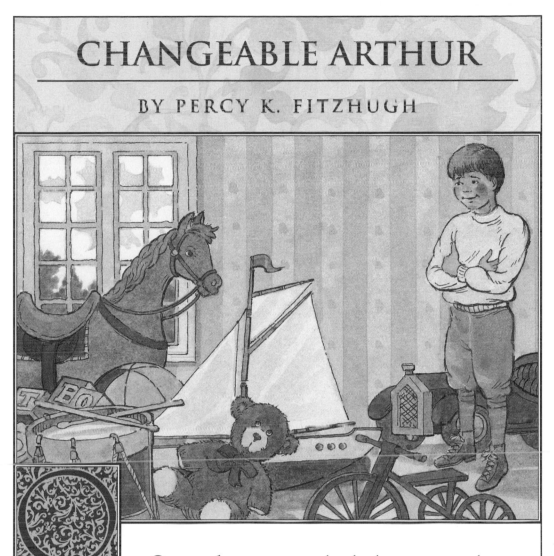

Once there was a little boy named Arthur who was always changing his mind. He was never happy, because he wanted things that other boys had and did not care for his own things. He had many nice toys, but he always thought that the toys of other boys were better.

Then as soon as his parents bought him something that he had asked for he would change his mind about it and wish for something else. So he was never very happy.

One day his uncle asked him what he was going to be when he grew up. Arthur said that he would like to be a druggist. He did not want to wait till he was grown up but wanted to be one right away. He was sure he would like it better than anything else in the world, because a druggist mixed things and had a funny pair of scales.

So his uncle told him that he would take him to a drug store where he knew the owner, and let him learn to be a real druggist. Arthur went in to the store very happy. He felt very proud when the druggist showed him the counter with all the medicine on it. But after Arthur had been a druggist for about an hour, he said that he was tired of that business and wanted to go home.

That night he told his uncle that he had changed his mind. Now he wanted to be an author and write books. He was sure he wouldn't change his mind again, for he had read many books and thought it must be nice to be a real author. His uncle smiled and got him a blank book and a pen. Arthur started to write a story about a giant. While he was writing, his father's donkey poked his head through the window with a knowing look as if he would like to have Arthur come out in the field and play. So Arthur went out to play with the donkey and forgot all about his story.

"Well," said his uncle that night, "how do you like being an author? You must let me read your story, Arthur."

Then Arthur turned very red and had to admit that he had forgotten all about wanting to be an author. His uncle smiled, and that night all the family went to a concert in the village where there was a band playing. On the way home Arthur said that he had at last made up his mind about what he would really like to be. A musician! If he could only learn to play the flute and then join a band, he would be happy for the rest of his life.

So the next night when his uncle came he brought him a tin flute and some sheets of music. Arthur played away on his flute all day until nearly suppertime. Then he got tired of it, and even his mother was tired of it, and everyone except Arthur's little puppies, who were very much interested.

When his uncle came that night he asked Arthur to bring his flute in and play a tune. But Arthur had lost the flute when he went out to play a little while before supper. And he had forgotten all about wanting to be a musician. He had to tell his uncle that he had changed his mind again. He was just going to say that he had decided to be a doctor when his uncle called him over and handed him a package.

"Now," said his uncle, "I want you to use this tomorrow, and at night you can tell me what you want next."

The package contained something that looked like a great big soup ladle with the spoon part made out of netting.

Arthur's father told him that it was to catch fish with. So he went out to a little brook not far away, and there he stayed all day fishing.

That night when his uncle came, Arthur ran up to him and thanked him for the new toy which he had so much fun with all day.

"Aren't you tired of it yet?" his uncle asked, for Arthur always became tired of a thing in one day.

"No, sir," said Arthur, "and I don't want to be any of the things that men are, but just a little boy and play out in the fresh air."

"Now, I will tell you something," said his uncle. "It is very nice to be a druggist or a musician or an author, but the best thing in the world to be is a contented little boy. And there isn't a musician or an author or a druggist that wouldn't be a little boy if he only knew how. For you can be those things a whole life long but you can only be a little boy once."

YOUNG PEOPLE, ENJOY YOURSELVES WHILE
YOU ARE YOUNG. BE HAPPY WHILE YOU ARE YOUNG.
ECCLESIASTES 11:9

WE THANK THEE

BY RALPH WALDO EMERSON

For flowers that bloom about our feet;
For tender grass, so fresh, so sweet;
For song of bird, and hum of bee;
For all things fair we hear or see,
Father in heaven, we thank Thee!

For blue of stream and blue of sky;
For pleasant shade of branches high;
For fragrant air and cooling breeze;
For beauty of the blooming trees,
Father in heaven, we thank Thee!

A MAN WITH A DREAM

BY ELIZABETH HARRISON

Once upon a time, far across the great ocean, there lived a little boy named Christopher. The city in which he lived was called Genoa. It was on the coast of the great sea, and from the time that little Christopher could first remember he had seen boats come and go across the water. I don't doubt that he had little boats of his own which he tried to sail or paddle about on the small pools near his home.

Soon after he was old enough to read books, he was given a book about the wonderful travels of a man named Marco Polo. Over and over again little Christopher read the marvelous stories told by this old traveler, of the strange cities and people that he had seen; of the strange houses; of the wild and beautiful animals that he had watched; of the jewels and perfumes and flowers which he had come across.

All day long the thoughts of little Christopher were busy with this strange far-away land which Marco Polo described. All night long he dreamed of the marvelous sights to be seen on those distant shores. Many times he went down to the water's edge to watch the ships as they slowly disappeared in the distance where the sea and the sky seemed to meet. He listened eagerly to everything about the sea and the voyages of adventure or trade, which were told by the sailors.

When he was fourteen years old, Christopher went to sea with an uncle, who was commander of one of the ships that came and went from the port of Genoa. For a number of years he lived on the ship, learning everything that he could about the sea. At one time the ship on which he was sailing had a fight with another ship; both ships caught on fire and were burned to the water's edge. Christopher Columbus escaped, as did the other sailors, by jumping into the sea and swimming to shore. Still this did not stop his love for ocean life.

After some time had passed, Christopher left Italy and went to live in Portugal, a land near the ocean. There he met and married a girl whose father had collected a large amount of maps and charts, which showed what was supposed to be the shape of the earth. The charts also told about strange and wonderful voyages, which brave sailors had dared to make into the unknown sea. Most people in those days thought it was certain death to any one who went too far out on the ocean.

There were all sorts of strange ideas about the shape of the earth. Some people thought it was round and flat like a pancake. They thought the waters that surrounded the land changed into mist and steam, and that whoever went through the mist fell off the edge of the earth. Others believed that there were huge monsters living in the distant waters, ready to swallow any sailor who was foolish enough to go out into those seas.

But Christopher Columbus had grown to be a very wise and thoughtful man. From the maps of his father-in-law, the books he read, and long talks with other learned men, he grew certain that the world was round like an orange. He believed that by sailing west from the coast of Portugal people could gradually go around the world to the land of Cathay. When he tried to explain why the earth was round and why he would not fall off, people shook their heads and thought he was crazy.

Christopher remembered in the book he read about Marco Polo that the people Marco met knew little about God and nothing about His Son. Since Christopher loved God, his mind was filled with the idea of going to this far-away land and telling the people about God and Jesus. The more he thought about it, the more he wanted to go, until his whole life was filled with the one thought of how to get some ships to prove that the earth was round and to go to these far-away lands to teach the people about God.

Through some friends he was given permission to see the King of Portugal. Eagerly he told the king of the great adventure which filled his heart. But the king was busy with other things and only listened to the words of Christopher as one might listen to the wind. Year after year passed, Columbus' wife died, and their one little son, Diego, was growing up. Finally Columbus decided he would leave Portugal and go to Spain to see if the king there would give him ships to make his trip.

The Spanish king was named Ferdinand, and the Spanish queen was a beautiful woman named Isabella. When Columbus told them of his belief that the world was round and of his desire to help the people who lived far away to know about God, they listened carefully to him. Both King Ferdinand and Queen Isabella were very honest people and wanted people everywhere to know about God and His Son. But their advisors persuaded them that the whole thing was a foolish

dream; and again Christopher was disappointed in his hope of getting help.

Still he did not give up. He sent his brother over to England to see if the English king would listen to him and help Christopher by giving him ships. But again, Christopher was disappointed as the English king would not help. Again and again Columbus tried to convince the Spanish king and queen that if they would help him, his discoveries would bring great honor and riches to their kingdom. They would also help the world by spreading the knowledge of Christ and God.

At last he decided to leave Spain. He took his son by the hand and walked a long way to a small seaport called Palos, where there was an old church. When he reached the gate of the church, he knocked on it and asked the man who answered if he could give Diego some water and bread. While the two tired travelers were resting on the steps, a man named Juan Perez came by and saw that these two people were not beggars. He invited them into the church and asked Columbus about his life. He listened quietly and thoughtfully to Columbus and his plan of crossing the ocean and telling the people about God.

Juan Perez had at one time been a very good friend of Queen Isabella's. After a long talk with Columbus, he borrowed a mule and rode for many miles across the open country to the palace to talk to the queen.

He returned on his mule to the old church and told Columbus to go back once more to the palace and talk to the queen. He told Christopher that there was no money to give him for his ships, but the queen now realized that it was a glorious thing Columbus wanted to do. She would sell her crown jewels for money so that Christopher could start on his dangerous journey.

This was important in those days, because queens were not considered dignified if they did not wear a crown of gold and jewels in public. But Queen Isabella cared far more about sending the gospel of Christ to other lands than about how she looked or what people might say. With a glad heart Columbus hurried back to the town of Palos where he had left his young son with Juan Perez.

Then a new problem arose. Columbus could not find enough sailors who would go on this voyage with him. Most of the sailors thought he was crazy and would not go on his ship. At last, the men from the prisons were given their freedom if they would go with Columbus on his ships. It was a tough crew that Columbus began with, but they were the best he could get.

His heart was so filled with the great work of God that he was willing to go on the voyage, no matter how many problems there might be. The ships were filled with food and other things that they would need for a long voyage. Nobody knew how long it would be before the land on the other side of the ocean would be reached.

Early one summer morning, even before the sun had risen, Columbus said goodbye to the few friends who had gathered at the seaport. The ships spread their sails and started on their voyage. The name of the largest ship was the Santa Maria, it was the one that Columbus himself commanded. The two smaller ships, were the Pinta and the Niña.

The sailors must have felt strange as hour after hour they drifted out into the great unknown waters where no man had ever gone before. Soon all land faded from their sight, and they sailed on. Columbus alone was filled with hope, feeling quite sure that in time he would reach the shores of a New World. On and on they sailed, day after day, far beyond the place where most sailors had been before.

Many of the men were filled with a strange feeling and pleaded to go home. Still they went on, each day taking them farther from all they had ever known. Days passed, and weeks until two months had gone by.

The food they had brought with them was getting low. The men grew angry with Columbus, and threatened to take his life if he did not command the ships to turn around and go back to Spain. But his patience and faith did not give out, and Christopher cheered the hearts of the men as best he could. He promised a rich reward for the first man to see land. This somewhat renewed their courage, and the men began to watch for land day and night. Flocks of birds flying westward began to be seen. This gave hope, for surely the birds must be flying toward some land where they could find food and trees in which to build their nests. Still many sailors were afraid, and Columbus knew that if land did not appear soon, his men could make him turn around whether he wanted to or not. He prayed that he would be given the courage to go on. Hour after hour he looked across the blue water, day and night, hoping to see land.

At last one night, as he sat on the deck on the ship, he thought he saw a faint light for a few moments in the distance. Where there is a light there must be land, he thought. Still he was not sure. So he asked one of the sailors to look out at the distance. Columbus then asked him what he saw. The sailor exclaimed, "A light, a light!"

Another sailor was called, but by this time the light had disappeared. So the sailor saw nothing, and Columbus' hopes sank again. About two o'clock that night the commander of one of the other ships started to shout, "Land ho! Land ahead!" You can imagine how much shouting there was and how the

sailors rushed to the edge of the ship to look for land. Early the next morning one of the sailors picked up a branch from a strange tree, and in the middle of the branch was a tiny bird's nest. This was sure evidence that they were near land, because branches of trees do not grow in water.

Little by little the land came in sight. About noon the next day, Columbus' ship came to ground upon the sand of the new country. No ship had ever touched this coast before.

At last, after a long life of working and studying, of hoping and planning, of trying and failing and trying yet again, Christopher Columbus realized his dream. He jumped from his ship onto the shore, and dropping to his knees, he kneeled and kissed the ground. Then he offered a prayer of thanks to God. Next the flag of Spain was planted in the land, and the newly discovered country was claimed in the name of King Ferdinand and Queen Isabella.

The great mystery of the ocean was known, and Columbus had reached a far distant country that none of his countrymen had even believed to exist. And he now knew that the whole round world could in time know about God.

THE CALF AND THE COLT

BY ROSEMARY SMITH

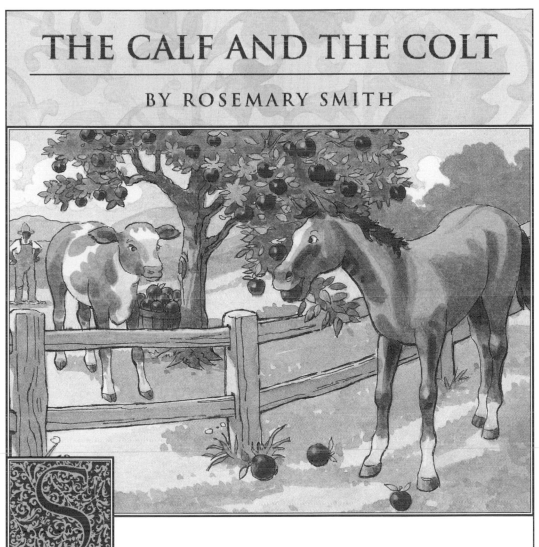

Strange things can happen when a colt and a calf meet each other under an apple tree. This time they made two old grouchy farmers very friendly again.

There was a big apple tree growing on the edge of Farmer Ryan's land. Its branches spread across the fence and hung over Farmer Jacob's land.

Now, Farmer Ryan did not like Farmer Jacob and Farmer Jacob did not like Farmer Ryan. The two men were always quarreling.

The animals on the two farms kept apart. Only Farmer Ryan's little calf and Farmer Jacob's little colt were friends. The calf and colt often met at the fence that separated the farms.

When the big apple tree was loaded with fruit, Farmer Ryan picked some of the apples and put them in a bushel basket. He left the basket near the tree, for he meant to come back and pick more fruit.

The calf was munching on one of the apples when his friend, the colt, came along. "Have an apple," said the calf, "they are delicious."

"Thank you," answered the colt. He stuck his head through the open space in the fence and got an apple. The two friends had quite a feast. The apples were very tasty.

While they were still eating, Farmer Ryan came back to the apple tree. Farmer Jacob happened along at the same time. "Your colt is eating my apples," cried Farmer Ryan angrily.

"Your calf is eating them; it is his fault," shouted Farmer Jacob.

The calf and colt were frightened. They huddled together, each shielding the other. The two men saw the animals trying to protect each other. Suddenly, they were ashamed of the way they were acting toward each other.

"You're welcome to some of the apples," said Farmer Ryan. "After all, part of the tree is on your land."

"Thank you," said Farmer Jacob. "I'm sorry I have been such a bad neighbor." And after that they were friends.

LOVE YOUR NEIGHBOR AS YOU LOVE YOURSELF.
LEVITICUS 19:18

THE RANSOM OF RED CHIEF

BY O. HENRY

It seemed like a good idea, but wait until I tell you what happened. We were down south, in Alabama, Bill and I, when this kidnapping idea struck us. It happened, as Bill said afterwards, "during a moment of temporary insanity," but we didn't know that until afterwards.

There was a town in Alabama called Summit. The people that lived there were trusting. Bill and I had six hundred dollars, and we needed two thousand dollars more for a plan we wanted to do in Illinois. We talked it over and decided that a kidnapping in Summit would be better than in a big town where reporters and state police could stir up all sorts of trouble. In Summit the worst that could happen was a few local policemen and lazy hounddogs would try to catch us.

We selected for our victim the only child of a prominent citizen named Ebenezer Dorset. The father was respectable and wealthy. The kid was a boy of ten with a face full of freckles, and orange hair. Bill and I figured that Ebenezer, the father, would hand over two thousand dollars without any questions to get his son back. But wait until I tell you what happened.

About two miles from Summit was a little mountain covered with trees. On the rear of this mountain was a cave. We put our supplies in there. The next evening after sundown, we rented a horse and buggy and drove past Dorset's house. The kid was in the street throwing rocks at a kitten on the opposite fence.

"Hey, little boy!" Bill yelled, "would you like to have a bag of candy and a nice ride?"

The boy turned and threw a rock, hitting Bill in the eye.

"That will cost his father an extra five hundred dollars," Bill said, climbing out of the buggy.

That boy put up a fight like a grizzly bear, but, at last, we got him into the bottom of the buggy and drove away. We took

him up to the cave, and I hitched the horse next to the trees.
After dark I drove the buggy back to the little village where had
we rented it, three miles away. And then I walked back to the
mountain cave.

Bill was putting ointment over his scratches and bruises.
There was a fire burning behind the big rock at the
entrance of the cave, and the boy was
watching a pot of boiling coffee. He
had two buzzard tail feathers stuck in
his red hair.

He pointed a stick at me when I
came up and said, "Ha! Paleface, do
you dare to enter the camp of Red
Chief, the terror of the plains?"

"He's all right now," said Bill,
rolling up his pants and looking at
some bruises on his shins. "We're
playing Indians. I'm old Hank, the
trapper, Red Chief's captive, and I'm to be scalped at daybreak.
Boy, that kid can kick hard!"

Yes, sir, that boy seemed to be having the time of his life.
The fun of camping out in a cave had made him forget that he
was a captive himself. He immediately named me Snake-eye,
the spy, and announced that I was to be burned at the stake at
the rising of the sun.

Then we had supper. He filled his mouth full of bacon and bread and gravy and began to talk.

"I like this fine. I never camped out before, but I had a pet 'possum once, and I was nine last birthday. I hate to go to school. Rats ate up sixteen of Jimmy Talbot's aunt's speckled hen's eggs. Are there any real Indians in these woods? I want some more gravy. Do the trees moving make the wind blow? We had five puppies. What makes your nose so red, Hank? My father has lots of money. Are the stars hot? I whipped Ed Walker twice Saturday. I don't like girls. You dassent catch toads unless with a string. Do oxen make any noise? Why are oranges round? Have you got beds to sleep on in this cave? Amos Murray has six toes. A parrot can talk, but a monkey or a fish can't. How many does it take to make twelve?"

Every few minutes he would remember that he was a pesky redskin, pick up his stick rifle, and tiptoe to the mouth of the cave to look for the scouts of the hated paleface. Now and then he would let out a war whoop that made old Hank the trapper shiver. That boy had Bill terrorized from the start.

"Red Chief," says I to the kid, "would you like to go home?"

"Aw, what for?" says he. "I don't have any fun at home. I hate to go to school. I like to camp out. You won't take me back home again, Snake-eye, will you?"

"Not right away," I said. "We'll stay here in the cave awhile."

"All right!" he said. "That'll be fine. I never had such fun in all my life."

We went to bed about eleven o'clock. We spread down some wide blankets and quilts and put Red Chief between us. We weren't afraid he'd run away. He kept us awake for three hours, jumping up and reaching for his rifle and screeching, "Hist! Pard," in mine and Bill's ears. At last I fell into a troubled sleep and dreamed that I had been kidnapped and chained to a tree by a ferocious pirate with red hair.

Just at daybreak, I was awakened by a series of awful screams from Bill. They weren't yells, or howls, or shouts, or whoops, such as you'd expect from a man. These were terrifying screams. It's an awful thing to hear a strong man scream in a cave at daybreak.

I jumped up to see what was the matter. Red Chief was sitting on Bill's chest with one hand in Bill's hair. In the other hand he had the sharp knife we used for slicing bacon, and he was trying to take Bill's scalp.

I got the knife away from the kid and made him lie down again. But, from that moment, Bill's spirit was broken. He laid down on his side of the bed, but he never closed an eye again in sleep as long as that boy was with us. I dozed off for a while, but along towards sun-up I remembered that Red Chief had said I was to be burned at the stake at the rising of the sun. I wasn't nervous or afraid, but I sat up and lit my pipe and leaned against a rock.

"What you getting up so soon for, Sam?" asked Bill.

"Me?" I said. "Oh, I've got a kind of pain in my shoulder. I thought sitting up would rest it."

"You're a liar!" said Bill. "You're afraid. You were going to be burned at the stake at sunrise, and you were afraid he'd do it. And he would, too, if he could find a match. Ain't it awful, Sam? Do you think anybody will pay money to get him back home?"

"Sure," I said. "A rowdy kid like that is just the kind that parents love. Now, you and the Chief get up and cook breakfast. I will go up on top of this mountain and think about our plan."

I went up on the peak of the little mountain and looked over the area. Over towards Summit I expected to see the men of the town armed with weapons looking for the kidnappers. But what I saw was a peaceful landscape, with one man ploughing with a mule. Nobody was looking in the creek, no men ran back and forth telling news of the kidnapping. There was a calm attitude about the town.

Perhaps, I said to myself, it has not yet been discovered that the little boy has been kidnapped. And I went down the mountain to breakfast.

When I got to the cave I found Bill backed up against the side of it, breathing hard, and the boy threatening to smash him with a rock half as big as a coconut.

"He put a hot boiled potato down my back," explained Bill, "and then mashed it with his foot. So I boxed his ears. Do you have a gun, Sam?"

I took the rock away from the boy and kind of patched up the argument.

"I'll fix you," said the kid to Bill. "No man has ever struck Red Chief and lived to tell about it. You better beware!"

After breakfast the kid took a piece of leather with strings wrapped around it out of his pocket and went outside the cave.

"What's he up to now?" Bill asked, anxiously. "You don't think he'll run away, do you, Sam?"

"No," I replied. "He doesn't seem to be much of a home body. But we've got to fix up some plan about the ransom. There doesn't seem to be much excitement around Summit because of his 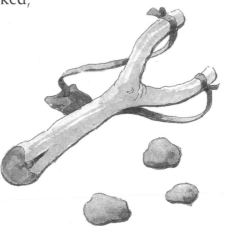 disappearance. But maybe they haven't realized he's gone yet. His folks may think he's spending the night with Aunt Jane or one of the neighbors. Anyhow, he'll be missed today. Tonight we must get a message to his father demanding the two thousand dollars for his return."

Just then we heard a kind of war whoop, such as David might have yelled when he knocked out the champion Goliath. It was a sling the Red Chief had pulled out of his pocket, and he was whirling it around his head.

I dodged, and heard a heavy thud and a kind of a sigh from Bill, like a horse gives out when you take his saddle off. A rock the size of an egg had caught Bill just behind his left ear. He shook himself all over and fell in the fire across the frying pan of hot water for washing the dishes. I dragged him out and poured cold water on his head for half an hour.

By and by, Bill sat up and felt behind his ear and said, "Sam, do you know who my favorite Bible character is?"

"Take it easy," I said. "You'll come to your senses presently."

"King Herod," he said. "You won't go away and leave me here alone, will you, Sam?"

I went out and caught that boy, and shook him until his freckles rattled.

"If you don't behave I'll take you straight home. Now, are you going to be good or not?"

"I was only having fun," he said sullenly. "I didn't mean to hurt Old Hank. But why did he hit me? I'll behave, Snake-eye, if you won't send me home, and if you'll let me play the Black Scout today."

"I don't know the game," I said. "That's for you and Mr. Bill to decide. He's your playmate for the day. I'm going away for awhile on business. Now, you come in and make friends with him and say you're sorry for hurting him, or home you go."

I made him and Bill shake hands, and then I took Bill aside and told him I was going to Poplar Grove, a little village three miles from the cave. I wanted to find out what I could about how the kidnapping had been regarded in Summit. Also, I thought it best to send a letter to Red Chief's father demanding the ransom and telling how it should be paid.

"You know, Sam," said Bill, "I've stood by you without batting an eye in earthquakes, fire and flood, in dynamite outrages, police raids, train robberies, and cyclones. I never lost my nerve yet till we kidnapped that two legged skyrocket of a kid. You won't leave me long with him, will you, Sam?"

"I'll be back some time this afternoon. You must keep the boy amused and quiet until I return. And now let's write the letter to his father."

Bill and I got some paper and a pencil and worked on the letter. Red Chief, with a blanket wrapped around him, was strutting up and down, guarding the entrance of the cave. Bill begged me tearfully to make the ransom fifteen hundred dollars instead of two thousand dollars, saying that it wasn't human for anybody to give up two thousand dollars for that forty pound chunk of freckled wildcat.

To relieve Bill, we compromised and wrote the letter this way·

Mr. Ebenezer Dorset:

We have your boy hidden in a place far from Summit. It is useless for you or the most skillful detectives to attempt to find him. Absolutely the only terms on which you can have him back are these: We demand fifteen hundred dollars in large bills for his return, the money is to be left at midnight tonight at the same spot and in the same box as your reply. If you agree to these terms, send your answer in writing by a messenger tonight at half past eight. After crossing Owl Creek on the road to Poplar Grove, there are three large trees about a hundred yards apart, close to the fence of the wheat field on the righthand side. At the bottom of the fence post, opposite the third tree, will be found a small cardboard box. The messenger will place the answer in this box and return immediately to Summit.

If you attempt any tricks or fail to agree to our demand as stated, you will never see your boy again.

If you pay the money as demanded, he will be returned to you safe and well within three hours. These terms are final, and if you do not agree to them, no further communication will be attempted.

Two Desperate Men

I addressed this letter to Dorset and put it in my pocket. As I was about to start, the kid came up to me and said, "Aw, Snake-eye, you said I could play the Black Scout while you are gone."

"Play it, of course," I said, "Mr. Bill will play with you. What kind of game is it?"

"I'm the Black Scout," said Red Chief, " and I have to ride to the stockade to warn the settlers that the Indians are coming. I'm tired of playing Indian myself. I want to be the Black Scout."

"All right," I said. "It sounds harmless to me. I guess Mr. Bill will help you trick the pesky savages."

Mr. Ebenezer Dorset
Summit

"What am I to do?" asked Bill, looking at the kid suspiciously.

"You are the horse," said Black Scout. "Get down on your hands and knees. How can I ride to the stockade without a horse?"

"You'd better keep him interested," I said, "until we get the plan going."

Bill got down on all fours, and a look came into his eye like a rabbit's when you catch it in a trap.

"How far is it to the stockade, kid?" he asked, in a husky manner of voice.

"Ninety miles," said Black Scout. "And you have to run to get there on time."

The Black Scout jumped on Bill's back and dug his heels into his side.

"Hurry back, Sam, as soon as you can," cried Bill. "I wish we hadn't made the ransom more than a thousand. Say, you quit kicking me, or I'll get up and warm you good."

I walked over to Poplar Grove and sat around the post office and store, talking with the local people that came in to trade. One fellow said that he heard Summit was all upset because of Ebenezer Dorset's boy having been lost or stolen. That was all I wanted to know. I bought some smoking tobacco, referred casually to the price of black-eyed peas, mailed my letter, and walked away. The postman said the mail carrier would come by in an hour and take the mail to Summit.

When I got back to the cave, Bill and the boy were not to be found. I explored the area around the cave and risked yelling for them, but there was no response.

So I lit my pipe and sat down to wait for them. In about half an hour I heard the bushes rustle. Bill waddled out in front of the cave. Behind him was the kid, stepping softly like a scout, with a broad grin on his face. Bill stopped, took off his hat, and wiped his face with a red handkerchief. The kid stopped about eight feet behind him.

"Sam," said Bill, "you'll think I'm a traitor, but I couldn't help it. The boy is gone. I sent him home. The plan is off."

"What's the trouble, Bill?" I asked.

"I was rode," said Bill, "the ninety miles to the stockade. Then, when the settlers were rescued, I was given oats. Sand isn't a very good substitute for oats. And then, for an hour I had to try to explain to him why there was nothing in holes, how a road can run both ways, and what makes the grass green. I tell you, Sam, a human can only stand so much. I took him and drug him down the mountain. On the way he kicked my legs black and blue from the knees down, and I've got two or three bites on my thumb and hand, but he's gone. Gone home. I showed him the road to Summit and kicked him about eight feet nearer there. I'm sorry we lose the ransom, but it was either that or Bill Driscoll would lose his mind."

Bill was puffing and blowing, but there was a look of peace and growing contentment on his face.

"Bill," I asked, "there isn't any heart disease in your family, is there?"

"No," replied Bill, "why?"

"Then you might turn around," I said, "and have a look behind you."

Bill turned and saw the boy. He turned white and sat down on the ground, beginning to pluck aimlessly at grass and little sticks. For an hour I was afraid he had lost his mind. Then I told him that my plan was to put the whole job through immediately, and we would get the ransom and be gone by midnight. So Bill braced up enough to give the kid a weak sort of a smile and a promise to play the Russian in a Japanese war with him as soon as he felt a little better.

I had a plan for collecting that ransom without danger of being caught by anyone. The tree under which the answer was to be left, and the money later on, was close to the road fence with big, bare fields on all sides. If anyone was watching the road, he would see him coming from a long way off. But at half past eight I was up in that tree as well hidden as a tree toad, waiting for the messenger.

Exactly on time, a half-grown boy rode up the road on a bicycle, found the cardboard box, and slipped a folded piece of paper into it. Then he pedaled back to Summit.

I waited an hour before I slid down the tree, got the note, slipped along the fence until I was in the woods, and was back at the cave in another half hour. I opened the note, got near the lantern, and read it to Bill. It was written with a pen, and the note said:

Two Desperate Men:

Gentlemen: I received your letter today by mail in regard to the ransom you ask for the return of my son. I think you are a little high in your demands, and I hereby make a counter offer, which I think you will accept. You bring Johnny home and pay me two hundred and fifty dollars in cash, and I agree to take him off your hands. You had better come at night, for the neighbors believe he is lost, and I couldn't be responsible for what they would do to anybody they saw bringing him back. Very respectfully,

Ebenezer Dorset

I glanced at Bill and saw that he had the most appealing look in his eyes I had ever seen.

"Sam," he said, "what's two hundred and fifty dollars, after all? We've got the money. One more night of this kid will send me to a mental hospital. You aren't going to let the chance go, are you?"

"To tell you the truth, Bill," I replied, "this little boy has gotten on my nerves too. We'll take him home, pay the ransom, and make our getaway."

We took him home that night. We got him to go by telling him that his father had bought a silver mounted rifle and a pair of moccasins for him, and we were to hunt bears the next day.

It was just twelve o'clock when we knocked at Ebenezer's front door. Just at the moment when I should have been taking the fifteen hundred dollars from the box under the tree, according to the original plan, Bill was counting out two hundred and fifty dollars into Dorset's hand.

When the kid found out we were going to leave him at home, he started to howl and fastened himself tightly onto Bill's leg. His father had to peel him away.

"How long can you hold him?" asked Bill.

"I'm not as strong as I used to be," said Dorset, "but I think I can promise you ten minutes."

"Enough," said Bill. "In ten minutes I shall cross the Central, Southern, and Middle Western States, and be running toward the Canadian border."

And, as dark as it was, and as fat as Bill was, and as good a runner as I am, he was a good mile and a half out of Summit before I could catch up with him.

PEOPLE WHO PLOW EVIL AND PLANT TROUBLE, HARVEST IT.
JOB 4:8

THE BOY WHO NEVER TOLD A LIE

Once there was a little boy,
  With curly hair and pleasant eye—
A boy who always told the truth,
  And never, never told a lie.

And when he trotted off to school,
  The children all about would cry,
"There goes the curly-headed boy—
  The boy that never tells a lie."

And everybody loved him so,
  Because he always told the truth,
That every day, as he grew up,
  'Twas said, "There goes the honest youth."

And when the people that stood near
  Would turn to ask the reason why,
The answer would be always this:
  "Because he never tells a lie."

THE FOX AND THE GRAPES

AN ÆSOP'S FABLE

One warm day a thirsty fox found some bunches of grapes growing high up on a vine. I must have those grapes, he thought. Again and again he jumped into the air but could not reach them.

At last he went away, saying, "The grapes are

very sour! Even the birds would not peck at them."

That is what people sometimes do when they cannot get what they want; they make believe that what they want is not good.

MORAL: BE HONEST WITH YOURSELF!

HOW MARGERY WONDERED

BY LUCY LARCOM

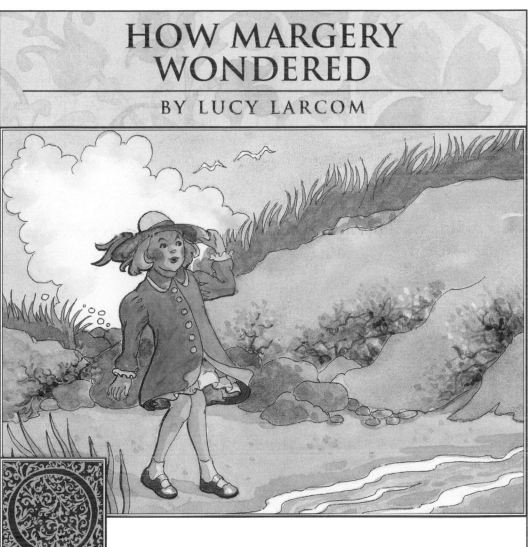

One bright morning late in March, little Margery put on her hat and her coat and went walking across the beach. It was the first time she had been trusted out alone, and she was very excited.

There was a pale mist on the far-off sea and

sky, and up around the sun were white clouds edged with pink and purple. The sunshine and the air made Margery's heart feel warm, and she let the soft wind blow her coat as she looked across the waters at the sun and wondered. For somehow, the sun had never looked before as it did today. It seemed like a great golden flower without a stem. Or was there a strong stem away behind it in the sky, that reached down below the sea to a root, and nobody could guess where?

Margery did not stop to find the answer to her question, as the tide was coming in and the waves were growing larger. Where did the waves come from? Who was down there under the blue wall of the horizon, with the strong voice pushing the water across the beach at her feet? And what secret was it they were whispering to each other? Oh, what was there beneath the sea, and beyond the sea, so deep, so big, way off where the big ships looked smaller than birds?

But while Margery stood still for a moment on dry rock and wondered, she heard a low, rippling cry from a tree on the cliff above her. It had been a long winter, and Margery had forgotten that there were birds and that birds could sing. So she wondered again what the music was.

And when she saw the bird perched on a brown branch, she wondered even more. It was only a bluebird, but it was the first bluebird Margery had ever seen. He fluttered among the twigs and looked as if he had grown out of them as the berries had.

But how did the music get in his throat? And after it was in his throat, how could it untangle itself and wind itself off so evenly? And from where had the bluebird flown?

The waves sang a welcome to him, and he sang a welcome to the waves. They seemed to know each other, and the ripple and warble sounded so much alike that the waves and the bluebird must have had the same music teacher. And Margery kept on wondering as she stepped between the song of the bluebird and the echo of the sea and climbed a bank just turning green in the spring sunshine.

The grass was beginning to grow. Margery knelt down closer to see the sharp points of new spears peeping from the ground. And scattered here and there were small, dark green leaves folded around buds shut up so tight that only those who had watched them for many seasons could tell that they would soon be flowers let out of their safe prisons. So no one could blame Margery for not knowing that they were only common things, or for stopping to look at the tiny buds, and wondering. What made the grass come up so green out of the black earth? And how did the flower buds know when it was time to take off their little green hoods and see what there was in the world around them? And how did they come to be buds at all? Did they bloom in another world before they sprung up here? Did they know what kind of flowers they should become? Had flowers souls, like little girls, that would live in another world when they died?

Margery thought she would like to sit down on the bank and wait beside the flower buds until they opened. Perhaps they would tell her their secret, if the very first thing they saw was her eyes watching them. One bud was beginning to unfold; it was streaked with yellow in little stripes that she could imagine became wider every minute. But she would not touch it, for it seemed almost as much alive as herself. She only wondered and wondered.

Margery heard her mother calling her, and she walked home across the shells and pebbles with a pleasant smile. For now she felt very much at home in this large, wonderful world and was happy to be alive, although she neither could have told, nor cared to know the reason why. But when her mother took off her coat and hat, Margery said, "Oh, mother, let's live on the doorstep. I think it would be nicer to live outside than inside. What makes everything so pretty and so happy? Don't you like to wonder?"

Margery's mother was a good woman, but she was busy with housework and did not often let her thoughts wander outside of the kitchen door. And just now she was baking some gingerbread, which was in danger of burning in the oven. So she put the coat and hat back on Margery and left her on the doorstep. Margery sat outside and wondered as the sea sounded louder, and the sunshine grew warmer around her. It was all so strange and grand and beautiful! Her heart danced with joy to the music that went through the wide world from the roots of the grass to the great golden blossom of the sun.

And when her round, gray eyes closed that night, the angels looked down and wondered over Margery. For the wisdom of the wisest being God has made ends in wonder; and there is nothing on earth so wonderful as the budding soul of a little child.

MORAL: NEVER STOP WONDERING,
FOR THROUGH WONDERING WE BECOME WISE.

THE LITTLE BOY WHO WASN'T LOST

BY JULILLY HOUSE KOHLER

Once there was a little boy named Peter who lived on a farm in the country. It wasn't a very big farm, but it was a nice one with fields and streams and woods near by to play in.

One summer day Peter said to his mother,

"Mother, this afternoon I want to pick blackberries in the woods."

"That would be nice," said his mother. "There's nothing your daddy loves better than a blackberry pie. Run along, but don't go too far in the woods and come home in time for supper."

So Peter took a berry pail and off he went toward the woods. First he crossed the road, looking very carefully in both directions to make sure there were no cars or hay wagons coming. Next he walked across Mr. Jensen's oat field. Then he squeezed, very carefully, under the barbed wire fence, and there he was at last, at the edge of the woods.

When he found the blackberries, they were dark and ripe. "Pling" went each fat berry as it slipped from its stem into Peter's pail. Sometimes there wasn't a "pling" because the berry went into Peter's mouth instead. The pail grew heavy and the sun was hot. Peter looked around for a place to cool off.

Down at the bottom of the hill was a stream. Peter raced toward it, and pulled off his shoes and socks before he waded into the cool water. Finally he went back to get his berry pail. "I have enough berries for the biggest pie in the world," he thought. Suddenly out of the bushes marched five baby pheasants. They were going for a walk all by themselves. Peter picked up his pail and started to follow the pheasants into the woods.

But baby pheasants can run fast, and in a few minutes Peter was deep in the woods and too tired to take another step. He threw himself down on some soft moss under a big tree and fell fast asleep.

When Peter awoke it was almost dark. The birds had stopped their chirping and the woods were very still. Peter felt around for his berry pail. He took a few steps one way, then he took a few steps another way. But he really did not know which way to go, so he sat down under the big tree again.

"There is no sense walking in the woods at night," he thought. "I'll just have to wait here for Daddy to come and take me home."

He was not the least afraid, for he knew exactly where he was. He was in the woods and the end of Mr. Jensen's oat field, across the road from his own farmhouse. His mother knew where he was and would tell his daddy, who would soon come and get him if he didn't come home for supper.

Just the same, Peter began to feel hungry. He thought of the blackberry pie that his mother was going to make. Then he began to think of all the other things that he liked to eat.

"Maybe if I say them out loud it will make me feel more cheerful," he thought to himself. So he took a deep breath and began.

"Hamburgers in crunchy buns, orange pop like at the circus, spaghetti with lots of cheese and tomatoes; and baked potatoes, bursting in the middle." His tummy gave a little groan, and he hurried to cheer it up some more.

"Corn on the cob, and lamb chops that you eat with your fingers, peach ice cream, oatmeal in the winter time, and chocolate cake; thick vegetable soup; carrots with lots of butter...."

"Carrots?" said a curious voice not two inches away from Peter's ear. "Did I hear somebody mention carrots?"

"Yes," said Peter in surprise, trying hard to see who was speaking to him, "I mentioned carrots."

"Shall we go and get some now? I was just about to start when I saw you sitting here."

"Who are you?" Peter asked, more surprised than ever. But he need not have asked, for at that very moment the big, round, cherry-colored moon rose full above the edge of the world and Peter could see who it was.

It was a big, gray rabbit!

"Why, you're a rabbit!" said Peter in amazement.

"Of course, I'm a rabbit," he said rather scornfully, "and you're a boy. Now shall we go get those carrots?"

"Well, I'm not sure that I'd better go with you," said Peter. "You see, I'm waiting for somebody to come find me."

"What do you mean 'find you'? I found you, didn't I? And besides," said the rabbit, "why do you have to be found? You know where you are, don't you?"

"Oh, yes, I know where I am. It's just that I don't know where my home is," said Peter. "You see, I came into the woods to pick blackberries...."

"Boys are silly," said the rabbit. "If they ate more carrots and less blackberries they could see better in the dark."

The rabbit looked at Peter, and Peter looked at the rabbit and for a moment neither one spoke. The moon was climbing high in the sky and the woods were becoming lighter. "All right," said Peter, and he smiled at the rabbit. "I will come with you and I do like carrots just as they grow, particularly if they are good ones."

"Good ones? These carrots are the best carrots in the country; and I should know. Come along, follow me." With a jump and a twist the big, gray rabbit ran away into the shadows so fast that Peter didn't even see which way he went.

"Wait!" he cried. "Wait for me! I must get my berry pail and I can't go as fast as you."

"Oh, of course," said the rabbit, bouncing back into a patch of moonlight. "I forgot, you're only a boy. I'll try to go more slowly."

The rabbit, however, scooted like lightning ahead of him, and hardly seemed to touch the ground. Peter hated to ask him to wait or to stop to rest, and did his best to keep up. But finally his shoes were so full of dirt and stones and sandy stuff that he felt he simply could not walk any further.

"Wait!" he called to the rabbit. "Oh, please wait just once more. You see, my shoes are full of stones and dirt and I think I'll just have to stop a minute to take them off and dump them out."

And Peter sat down and tugged and tugged and finally got his shoes off and poured simply buckets of stuff out of them. The gray rabbit sat and looked at him. But all he said was "Boys!"

After that, it wasn't so bad. They reached the end of the field and walked on solid grass for a while and then, for some reason, they stopped. Only this time, it was the rabbit who stopped.

"Now here," said the rabbit sounding rather scared, "this is the most dangerous place on the whole trip. On this enormous, hard path are monsters roaming."

"Monsters?" said Peter.

"Monsters," repeated the rabbit. "Tremendous monsters with eyes as big as moons that shoot fiery lights as they look for you. Look out! Here comes one now."

Peter looked and what he saw made him grin and then giggle. "Silly!" he said. "Those aren't monsters. Those are automobiles. Those are not eyes shooting fire, they are headlights."

When they had crossed the road, with Peter's help, the rabbit said, "Well, we're here at last. And I for one, think it's about time. Just follow me and don't make a noise, and in a few minutes we'll be at the carrots. I can smell them already. Look! There they are just waiting for us. I'll take this row and you can take the next."

And the only thing Peter heard after that was a pawing and a nibbling and a munching, as the hungry gray rabbit settled down to his feast. But Peter didn't so much as bend down and pull one crisp carrot. Peter just stood there and looked all around and strained his eyes to see in the moonlight.

"Rabbit," he said softly, "Rabbit, are there, by any chance, beans growing in the next row to this?"

"Don't bother with them. They are old and woody and the new ones are just coming up," said the rabbit with his mouth full of carrot.

"Rabbit," Peter went on and he began to sound very excited, "Rabbit, are there big onions in the row next to the beans?"

"Onions? Yes, there are, but who would want onions?" asked the rabbit.

"I would. Oh, I would!" shouted Peter. "I would want onions and beans and carrots because I planted them and I am home!"

And he began to run as fast as he could toward his house. Just as he reached the front steps, the door swung open and

there stood his mother and daddy, and his daddy had a big flashlight in his hand.

"Mother," said Peter, "I didn't mean to go too far or stay too late, and I brought the blackberries for Daddy's pie, and a rabbit brought me home and is eating carrots this very minute in my garden."

"I know," said his mother softly. "I know, and when he gets through with the carrots in your garden, he is welcome to the carrots in mine."

"I like blackberry pie much better, anyway," said his daddy. And they all went into the warm, pleasant house and closed the door behind them.

BE STRONG AND BRAVE.
DON'T BE AFRAID.
THE LORD YOUR GOD WILL BE WITH
YOU EVERYWHERE YOU GO.
JOSHUA 1:9

THE STEAMBOAT AND THE LOCOMOTIVE

BY GELETT BURGESS

On the railway that ran through the city of Ligg there was once a locomotive who was always discontent and grumbling. Nothing in the world was good enough for him; or at least, nothing in the city of Ligg. His coal was too hard or too soft; it was never just right.

He hated to pull passenger trains because he had to go so fast, and he didn't like to pull freight trains because they were too heavy. He was always complaining that he was out of order, so that he might stay in the roundhouse, and not work. He was afraid to go over bridges, for fear they would break down and he hated tunnels because they were so dark and cold. He thought iron rails were too soft to get a good hold of, and he said the steel rails were altogether too slippery. Sometimes he declared that he wouldn't run where there were not modern metal ties, and at other times he said that the old fashioned wooden ties made a much better road. He quarreled with his tender, and he refused to be hooked up to another car he didn't like. He snorted and hissed at the semaphores and point signals, and he was a nuisance to the railway in more ways than can be told.

But if you think he was bad, there was a young steamboat on the river that was worse. She was a very pretty craft, but that was no reason why she should insist on having a new set of paddle wheels every year. She was very particular about her funnel, and if it were not painted the exact color that she fancied, she would declare that she would scuttle herself. She would roll and pitch with anger if they tried to back her. She would dig up the muddy bottom of the river with her paddles, and she gave a great deal of trouble about the steering.

When these ill-natured creatures came together at the dock in the river, below the fortifications, they used to complain to each other till the bridge told them they ought to be ashamed of themselves.

One day, after the steamboat had been carrying a load of noisy passengers up from the harbor, she found the locomotive on the pier in a very gloomy state of mind.

"I'm not going to stand this any longer!" he said. "They've put me to hauling coal, and it's no work for a machine like me, especially when I can't burn any of it myself. I'm going to run away!"

"Well, that is a good idea; suppose I go with you, and we'll set out together to seek our fortunes!" said the steamboat.

They talked it all over, and finally decided to start that very night. The steamboat was to help the locomotive on the water, and the locomotive was to help the steamboat on the land. They were to share their wood and coal and water together, and have a very good time as long as they could.

At midnight the locomotive got on board the boat, and she steamed softly up the river. "This is fun!" said the locomotive.

"It's all right for you," said the boat, "but you're heavier than I thought. Wait till it's your turn to give me a ride. I can't go much farther, anyway, the water is getting shallow. There is a dam up above here, so I think we had better go ashore now."

She climbed up the bank with the locomotive's help, and he then lifted her up on top of his cab, and set out across the fields. She was a little boat but she was heavy, and the locomotive puffed away with all his might through the grass, stopping to rest once in a while. So they went on for several days, taking turns carrying each other.

After awhile they began to approach a line of hills, and the ground grew steeper and steeper, till at last the locomotive could go no further with the steamboat on his back. So she got off the scrambled along for a few miles with her paddle wheels while the locomotive pushed her from behind. But the time came when neither of them could go a step further, and they lay on the ground exhausted. To make matters worse, they grew short of water and fuel. They cut down their rations to a ton of coal and a barrel of water a day, and even then they didn't have enough to take them back to either a forest or a lake.

It seemed likely that they would have to perish there on the hillside, and they quarreled with each other, each accusing the other of being at fault for suggesting this terrible journey. The old river and the city of Ligg had never seemed so pleasant before, but it was many days journey from here.

Just as they had begun to think that all hope was gone, the steamboat saw a dot in the sky. It slowly grew bigger and bigger as they watched it.

"It is a balloon!" they both cried together, and they began to blow their whistles with all their strength.

The balloon came near, till it was close enough for them to see that it was laughing. The balloon was very fat, pink and round, and it shook with merriment as its basket swung above them.

"Well, I declare!" the balloon cried out. "This is the strangest thing I ever saw. What are you doing way up in these mountains? I never saw a locomotive or a steamboat on top of a hill before."

"Please don't laugh at us," cried the steamboat. "Help us come down."

The balloon said that he would help them over the mountains, and let down a rope, which the two tied around their waists. The balloon then rose, and the locomotive and the steamboat were lifted high in the air. They sailed away towards the East, across the tops of the mountains. They had floated for half a day like this, when the balloon gave a pull and the rope suddenly broke!

Down went the two, falling faster and faster through the air. But they landed safely in an oak tree in the middle of a forest, without breaking any machinery.

Even though they were out of the mountains, they were now lost and did not know which way to go.

The locomotive finally succeeded in climbing a tall tree and saw some smoke rising in the distance. They decided to walk towards the smoke, hoping that they could find some help. After they had walked awhile they came to an old sawmill by the side of a little stream. It was an ugly and dark old mill that scared them both. But this was their only hope for help, so they decided to go closer to the mill.

The mill welcomed them, but there was something in his dusty, oily manner that the locomotive did not trust, and he decided to stay awake and watch. The little steamboat was too tired to notice anything. And after they had drunk many barrels of water each and eaten a few tons of sawdust, which was all the mill could offer them, they felt better.

Not too long after they had burned the last mouthful, they both fell into a deep sleep and knew nothing for many hours. A pain in his side suddenly awakened the locomotive. He jumped up, but it was too late, his left side wheel had been sawed off. He ran at the sides of the mill, and tore open a big hole, then dragged out the steamboat and ran with her into the forest.

In the morning after a short sleep, they awoke to find themselves by the side of a wide river. Alongside the bank of the river ran a beautiful level railway line.

It did not take them long to decide what to do. The little steamboat gave one leap into the river, and whistled long and happily. The locomotive crawled onto the line, and rang its bell with a joyful clang. For they knew by the looks of the country that they had been travelling in a large circle, and the river and the railway led directly to the city of Ligg.

So they steamed along, side by side, together, the lame locomotive and the shamefaced steamboat. That day one laid her head at last alongside the dock, and one puffed timidly into the station; both decided never to complain of any work that they should have to do in the future.

I HAVE LEARNED TO BE SATISFIED WITH THE THINGS
I HAVE AND WITH EVERYTHING THAT HAPPENS.
PHILIPPIANS 4:11

YOU MUSTN'T QUIT

When things go wrong, as they sometimes will,
When the road you're trudging seems all uphill,
When the funds are low and the debts are high
And you want to smile, but you have to sigh,
When care is pressing you down a bit,
Rest! if you must—but never quit.

Life is strange, with its twists and turns,
As every one of us sometimes learns,
And many a failure turns about
When he might have won if he'd stuck it out,
Stick to your task, though the pace seems slow—
You may succeed with one more blow.

Success is failure turned inside out—
The silver tint of the clouds of doubt—
And you never can tell how close you are,
It may be near when it seems afar;
So stick to the fight when you're hardest hit—
It's when things seem worst that YOU MUSTN'T QUIT.

NELLIE'S WISH

BY ARTHUR MAXWELL

School was over. The holidays had begun. Everyone was looking forward to Christmas Day. How slowly the time seemed to pass! It seemed as if Christmas would never come. Outdoors it was too cold to play, and indoors there seemed nothing to do without getting in mamma's way. "Oh, what shall we do?" said Nellie to her little sister Elsie.

"Let's write that letter to Santa Claus we were going to send him."

"If you like," said Nellie. "But do you know I believe Santa Claus is Daddy dressed up."

"Do you?"

"Yes. Last Christmas I kept one eye open till someone came into my room to fill my stocking, and I'm sure it was daddy in his bathrobe."

"Let's write the letter, anyway, just to be sure," urged little Elsie.

"Oh, yes, that will be fun. What shall we ask him to send us?"

"Let's get some paper and a pencil first, so we won't forget anything."

"I'll run and get some," said Nellie, and off she went, coming back in a few minutes with enough paper for a very long letter.

Since Elsie had just learned to write, it was agreed that she should write the letter, while Nellie sat by to tell her how to spell the words.

"Before you begin, let's try to think of what we would like most," said Nellie.

So they talked it over very seriously, and came to the conclusion that they wanted a large number of things. Elsie was sure she needed a box of paints, a baby doll, a doll buggy, a ball, lots of candy, oranges, and apples, and a music box. Nellie had bigger ideas. She wanted a bike, some picture books, a big box of chocolate candy, and above all else, a doll that could talk and close its eyes.

"I really don't think he will be able to carry them all," said Nellie.

"Oh, I do," said Elsie. "He has a big bag."

"Yes, and there is no harm in putting them all down."

So they did. Being very careful as she wrote, Elsie wrote the letter, underlining all the things they especially wanted. At last the letter was finished and ready to be placed in an envelope. Nellie read it over, all the way from "Dear Santa Claus" down to "Hoping to see you soon." Then she gave a little sigh.

"Why, what's the matter?" asked Elsie.

Nellie was silent a moment. Then she said, "I think is it is a rather selfish letter."

"Why?"

"Because we have asked for things only for ourselves. There's not one thing for anyone else."

"You're right. What should we do? Will we need to write the letter all over again?"

"Oh, no; that would take too long. Why not add a postscript."

"What's that?"

"Just a few words at the bottom."

"All right. What should we say?"

"I would like to see some of the other children at school get some nice things like those we have asked for."

"So would I."

"There's Kittie Gordon," said Nellie. "She's such a nice girl, but her mother is so poor that I don't think she will get any

Christmas presents."

"Won't she really?"

"I don't think so."

"Then let's ask for something nice to be taken to her. I'm sure she would like a pretty doll, too."

"Yes," said Nellie. "Let's write that down. Then the letter will be all right, I think."

So Elsie carefully added the words, "Please see that Kittie Gordon gets a beautiful doll." Then they folded up the letter, put it in the envelope, stuck a stamp on it, and handed it to their mother, asking her to mail it for them.

Christmas morning came, and with it all the glorious fun of opening the stockings and examining the presents that were piled up beside their beds. Nellie and Elsie were as happy as children could be, shrieking with delight as each package was opened and they found something for which they had asked in their letter. Of course they did not get everything that they had asked for; but it seemed as if they has been sent the things they wanted most of all.

But there was one thing wrong, at least so far as Nellie was concerned. She did not say anything about it till she had opened all her packages. Then she began to look just a little bit worried. She turned all the tissue paper over again and again and looked under the bed, even in the closet, but in vain. The thing she wanted most of all was not there.

"What's the matter, Nellie?" asked Elsie. "Haven't you got

enough things?"

"Oh, Elsie," said Nellie, "I know I have some very nice things, but it is not here."

"What do you mean?"

"Oh, I really did want a doll."

"Maybe Santa took one to Kittie Gordon instead of you."

"Perhaps so," sighed Nellie. "But I didn't really mean him to do that."

Hardly had she said it when she realized how really mean it was. She had all these beautiful things, and most likely Kittie had nothing. All day she felt unhappy about it, and in the midst of all the play with her new toys, she kept thinking of her friend Kittie.

In the evening Nellie and Elsie went out to a party that was being given by the people next door. There were several other little girls there, and they had a fine time together.

After refreshments they all went into another room, and in the center of the room was a tall Christmas tree covered with presents and little colored lights. It was very pretty to look at. But the thing which took Nellie's attention the most was the beautiful doll perched right on the top of the tree. Her heart beat fast as she thought that perhaps now her great wish was to be granted. They played all kinds of games near the tree, and at last the presents were distributed. Only one thought was in Nellie's mind—who was going to get the doll?

Impatiently she waited and waited while every other child

received a gift. Now there was just one thing left on the tree. It was the doll.

"This," said the lady, "is for—"

"Nellie," said all the children, for they saw that she had nothing from the tree so far.

Nellie blushed and jumped up from her seat. Taking the doll from the lady, she hugged it tightly to herself while everybody clapped.

Then a strange thing happened. Nellie was walking back to her seat when suddenly she turned quite white and, pointing to the window, cried, "Oh, look!"

Everybody looked, but there was nothing to be seen. The shades were up, but outside all was dark and still.

"What was it?" cried all the children.

"It was Kittie Gordon. She was looking in through the window, and I'm sure she had been crying. Oh, I must go at once to see!"

And without another word Nellie rushed to the front door and ran out without waiting to put on her coat. Far down the street, under a light, Nellie thought she saw a little figure.

"Kittie!" she cried out. "Kittie! Come here."
But Kittie went on, and Nellie had to run the whole length of the street before she caught up with her.

"Oh, Kittie," she panted, "I have brought you something. Please do stop and take it."

Kittie stood there in the street looking in amazement at the wonderful thing she held in her arms. It was a doll that could shut its eyes and say, "Mamma."

"For me?" she asked.

"Yes, yes, for you," replied Nellie. "I want you to have it most of all." Then she turned and ran back to the house, feeling happier than she had ever felt in all her life.

MORAL: THE BEST GIFTS ARE THOSE THAT YOU GIVE
FROM YOUR HEART.

BRER RABBIT AND THE BAG FULL OF TURKEYS

BY JOEL CHANDLER HARRIS

One day Brer Rabbit was sitting under a tree, thinking about what he was going to do next. He just couldn't make up his mind. On one hand he was feeling a little hungry, but on the other hand he was feeling sort of lazy. And he wasn't in the mood to scurry around and get himself something to eat. In a little while Brer Bear came along with a big empty sack slung over his shoulder.

"Howdy, Brer Bear! Where are you going with that sack?" called out Brer Rabbit.

"I am going hunting. So long!" And having said that Brer Bear went walking off on his way.

Brer Rabbit just grinned. Now he knew that he wasn't going to be hungry for too long. And he also knew that he wouldn't have to scurry around to get himself something to eat.

Well, for the rest of the day until the sun went down Brer Rabbit just laid around being lazy. Then he got up and climbed a tree to watch for Brer Bear coming back from hunting. He hadn't been watching very long when he saw Brer Bear coming tromping through the woods with his hunting bag full of wild turkeys.

Brer Rabbit jumped down from the tree. He scampered through the bushes, and he came out at a place on the road where Brer Bear was bound to pass by. Then he began to work. First, he pulled a twig off one of the bushes. He took out his knife and he cut the twig into the shape of an arrow. Next, he took off his clothes and hid them under the tall grass. Of course, without his own shirt, and without his own pants Brer Rabbit didn't look like Brer Rabbit at all. He looked like any other ordinary rabbit in the world.

Now Brer Rabbit lay down on the ground. Then he put the arrow against his side so that it looked like it was stuck right through his heart. Then he stretched out straight and stiff, exactly like he was dead.

Pretty soon along came Brer Bear. When he saw a rabbit lying on the ground with an arrow sticking through him, he stopped and took a look.

"Mmmm," he said to himself, "somebody must have shot this rabbit. Mmmm, such a fine, fat rabbit!" Brer Bear licked his lips. Then he looked down at his hunting bag filled up with wild turkeys. "Too bad I don't have room for this rabbit. Oh well, I don't!" He sighed and walked on down the road.

Soon as Brer Bear was out of sight, up jumped Brer Rabbit. Off he scampered through the woods, and he came out at another place on the road where Brer Bear was bound to pass by. Again he lay down on the ground. Again he put the arrow against his side, and stretched out like he was dead.

In a little while along came Brer Bear. "My, my!" he said. "Another rabbit. And just as fat as the first one." He looked at Brer Rabbit a minute and his mouth began to water. Then he slung his bag of turkeys down from his shoulder and dropped it on the ground. "These fat rabbits are going to waste. I can't allow that. I'll just leave my turkeys here a minute, while I go back and get the other rabbit. Then I'll string the two rabbit together, and I'll just drag them the rest of the way home."

Brer Bear marched back down the road toward the place where he saw the first rabbit.

Scarcely was Brer Bear out of sight, when Brer Rabbit jumped up. He grabbed the bag full of turkeys, and off he pranced lippity-clippity, grinning and chuckling and laughing big laughs.

And Brer Bear went home without his turkeys, and without his two fat rabbits, and he never did find out who stole them.

DON'T MAKE PLANS TO HURT YOUR NEIGHBOR.
HE LIVES NEARBY AND TRUSTS YOU.
PROVERBS 3:29

PUDDLEBY

BY HUGH LOFTING

Once upon a time, many years ago when our grandfathers were little children there was a doctor; and his name was Dolittle. He lived in a little town called Puddleby-on-the-Marsh. All the folks, young and old, knew him and whenever he walked down the street everyone would say, "There goes the doctor. He's a clever man."

The house he lived in on the edge of the town was quite small, but his garden was very large and wide with stone benches and weeping willow trees. His sister, Sarah Dolittle, was housekeeper for him, but the doctor looked after the garden himself.

He liked animals and kept many kinds of pets. Besides the goldfish in the pond in his garden, he had rabbits in the pantry, white mice in his piano, a squirrel in the linen closet, and a hedgehog in the cellar. He had a cow with a calf and an old lame horse and chickens and pigeons and two lambs and many other animals. But his favorite pets were Dab-Dab the duck, Jip the dog, Gub-Gub the baby pig, Polynesia the parrot, and the owl Too-Too.

His sister used to grumble about all these animals and said they made the house untidy. And one day when a lady who was sick came to see the doctor, she sat on the hedgehog who was sleeping on the sofa and was so surprised that she never came to see the doctor any more. But drove every Saturday all the way to Oxenthorpe, another town ten miles away to see a different doctor.

Then his sister, Sarah Dolittle, came to him and said, "How can you expect sick people to come and see you when you keep all these animals in the house? It's a fine doctor who would have his house full of hedgehogs and mice. That is the fourth person these animals have driven away. Many have said they wouldn't come near your house again, no matter how sick they are. We are getting poorer every day. If you go on like this, none of the people will have you for a doctor."

"But I like the animals better than the people," said Doctor Dolittle.

So as time went on, the doctor got more and more animals; and the people who came to see him got less and less. Till at last he had no one left, except the cat's meat man who wasn't very rich and only got sick once a year at Christmastime.

But the doctor kept on getting more pets, and of course it cost a lot to feed them. And the money he had saved up grew littler and littler. Then he sold his piano, and let the mice live in a bureau-drawer. But the money he got for that began to go; so he sold the brown suit he wore and went on becoming poorer and poorer.

And now when he walked down the street people would say to one another, "There goes Dr. Dolittle. There was a time when he was the best doctor in the country. But look at him now, he hasn't any money and his socks are full of holes."

But the dogs and the cats and the children still ran up and followed him through the town, the same as they had done when he was rich.

MORAL: DON'T JUDGE OTHERS BY THEIR APPEARANCE.

SMILES

BY ARTHUR MAXWELL

A smile is quite a funny thing;
It wrinkles up your face;
And when it's gone, you cannot find
Its secret hiding place.
But far more wonderful is
To see what smiles can do.
You smile at one, he smiles at you,
And so one smile makes two.
He smiles at someone, since you smiled,
And then that one smiles back;
And that one smiles until in truth
You fail in keeping track.
And since a smile can do great good
By cheering hearts of care,
Let's smile and smile, and not forget
That smiles go everywhere!

MR. TOAD'S OLD SUIT

BY THORTON W. BURGESS

P Peter Rabbit was tired and very sleepy as he hopped along the crooked little path down the hill. He could see old Mother West Wind just emptying her Merry Little Breezes out of her big bag onto the Green Meadows to play all the bright summer day.

Peter Rabbit yawned and yawned again as he watched them dance over to the Smiling Pool. Then he hopped on down the crooked little path toward home.

Sammy Jay, sitting on the fence post, saw him coming. "Peter Rabbit, out all night! Oh, my goodness, what a sight! Peter Rabbit, reprobate, no good end will be your fate!" shouted Sammy Jay.

Peter Rabbit stuck his tongue out at Sammy Jay and shouted back, "Who stole Happy Jack's nuts: Thief! Thief! Thief!"

It was true, Peter Rabbit had been out all night playing in the moonlight, stealing a midnight feast in Farmer Brown's cabbage patch, and getting into mischief with Bobby Coon. Now when most of the little meadow people were just waking up, Peter Rabbit was thinking of bed.

Presently he came to a big piece of bark, which was the roof of Mr. Toad's house. Mr. Toad was sitting in his doorway blinking at Mr. Sun, who had just begun to climb the sky.

"Good morning, Mr. Toad," said Peter Rabbit.

"Good morning," said Mr. Toad.

"You're looking very fine this morning, Mr. Toad," said Peter Rabbit.

"I'm feeling very fine this morning," said Mr. Toad.

"Why, you have on a new suit, Mr. Toad!" exclaimed Peter Rabbit.

"Well, what if I have, Peter Rabbit?" demanded Mr. Toad.

"Oh, nothing, nothing at all, Mr. Toad," said Peter Rabbit,

"Only I didn't know you ever had a new suit. What have you done with your old suit, Mr. Toad?"

"Swallowed it," said Mr. Toad shortly, turning his back on Peter Rabbit.

That was all Peter Rabbit could get out of Mr. Toad. So he started on down the crooked little path. Now Peter Rabbit has a great deal of curiosity and is forever poking into other people's business. The more he thought about it, the more he wondered what Mr. Toad could have done with his old suit. Of course he hadn't swallowed it!

"I'll just run over to the Smiling Pool and ask Grandfather Frog. He'll surely know what Mr. Toad does with his old suits," said Peter Rabbit and began to hop faster.

When he reached the Smiling Pool, there sat Grandfather Frog on his big green lily pad as usual. There was a hungry look in his eyes, for it was too early for green flies to have come by him. But Peter Rabbit was too full of curiosity in Mr. Toad's business to notice that Grandfather Frog was hungry, and help him.

"Good morning, Grandfather Frog," said Peter Rabbit.

"Good morning," replied Grandfather Frog, a little bit gruffly.

"You're looking very fine this morning, Grandfather Frog," said Peter Rabbit.

"Not so fine as I'd feel if I had a few fat, foolish, green flies," said Grandfather Frog.

"I've just met your cousin Mr. Toad, and he has on a new suit," said Peter Rabbit.

"Indeed!" replied Grandfather Frog. "Well, I think it's about time."

"What does Mr. Toad do with his old suit, Grandfather Frog?" asked Peter Rabbit.

"Chug-a-rum! It's none of my business. Maybe he swallows it," replied Grandfather Frog crossly, and turned his back on Peter Rabbit.

Peter Rabbit saw that his curiosity must remain unsatisfied. He suddenly remembered that he had been out all night and was very sleepy. So he started off home across the Green Meadow.

Now the Merry Little Breezes had heard all that Peter Rabbit and Grandfather Frog had said, and they decided that they would find out from Grandfather Frog what Mr. Toad really did with his old suit. First they scattered over the Green Meadows. Then they all came back, each blowing a fat, foolish, green fly towards Grandfather Frog's lily pad.

"Chug-a-rum!" said Grandfather Frog, as each fat, foolish, green fly disappeared inside his white-and-yellow vest. The last one was out of sight, all but a leg which was left sticking out of a corner of Grandfather Frog's big mouth. So one of the Merry Little Breezes asked him what became of Mr. Toad's old suit.

Grandfather Frog settled comfortably on the big green lily pad and folded his hands across his white-and-yellow vest.

"Chug-a-rum," began Grandfather Frog. "Once upon a time...."

The Merry Little Breezes clapped their hands and settled themselves among the daisies. They knew that soon they would know what Mr. Toad did with his old suit.

"Once upon a time," began Grandfather Frog again, "old King Bear received word that a special visitor would be coming to see Green Meadows and the Green Forest. Of course, old King Bear wanted his kingdom and his subjects to look their very best. So he issued a royal order that everyone of the little Meadow people and everyone of the Forest folk should wear a new suit on the day that the visitor was to come.

"Now, like old King Bear, everyone wanted to appear his very best before the special visitor. But no one knew the exact day she was to come. So everyone began to wear his best suit every day and to take the best care of it. Old King Bear appeared every day in a suit of shining black. Lightfoot, the deer, threw away his dingy gray suit and put on a coat of beautiful red and tan. Mr. Mink, Mr. Otter, Mr. Muskrat, Mr. Rabbit, Mr. Woodchuck, Mr. Coon, who you know was first cousin to Old King Bear, Mr. Gray Squirrel, Mr. Fox Squirrel, Mr. Red Squirrel, all put on brand new fur suits. Mr. Skunk changed his black-and-white stripes for a suit of all black, very handsome indeed. Mr. Chipmunk took care to see that his new suit had all the most beautiful stripes.

"Mr. Jay, who was something of a showoff, had a wonderful new coat. It looked as if it had been cut from the bluest patch of sky and trimmed with edging taken from the whitest clouds. Even Mr. Crow and Mr. Owl tried to look their best.

"But Mr. Toad couldn't see the need for such a fuss. He thought his neighbors spent too much time and thought on how they looked. Oh, he wanted to look his best when the special visitor came, so he got a new suit, too. But Mr. Toad couldn't afford to sit around doing nothing so that his new clothes would stay nice. No indeed! Mr. Toad had too much to do. He was too busy taking care of a large garden, and garden work is hard on clothes. So Mr. Toad just wore his old suit over his new one and went about his business.

"Soon the day came when the special visitor arrived to see the kingdom of old King Bear. All the little Meadow people hurried to say hello to the visitor and to show off their new clothes, all but Mr. Toad. He was so busy that he didn't even know that the visitor had arrived.

"Late in the afternoon, Mr. Toad stopped to rest. He had just cleared his cabbage patch of the slugs that threatened to eat up his crop, and he was very tired. Presently he happened to look up the road, and who should he see but the visitor coming to see his garden.

"Suddenly Mr. Toad remembered that he had on his working clothes, which were very old and very dirty. For just a minute he didn't know what to do. Then he dove under a cabbage leaf and began to pull off his old suit. But the old suit stuck! He was in such a hurry and so excited that he couldn't find the buttons. Finally he got his pants off. Then he reached over and got hold of the back of his coat. He tugged and pulled until finally he pulled his old coat off right over his head just as if it were a shirt.

"Mr. Toad gave a great sigh of relief as he stepped out in his new suit. You remember that he had been wearing that new suit underneath the old one all the time.

"Mr. Toad was very happy with himself until he thought how terribly untidy that ragged old suit looked lying on the ground. What should he do with it? He couldn't hide it in the garden, for the visitor would be sure to see it. What should he do?

"Then Mr. Toad had a thought. Everyone made fun of his big mouth. But what was a big mouth for if not to use? He would swallow his old suit! In a flash Mr. Toad jumped under a cabbage leaf and crammed his old suit into his mouth.

"When the visitor came into the garden, Mr. Toad was waiting in the path to say hello. He looked very nice in his new suit. You would have thought he had been waiting all day like that. Except for one thing, swallow as much and as hard as he could, he couldn't quite get down all of his old suit. A leg of his pants hung out from a corner of his big mouth.

"Of course, the special visitor saw it right away and laughed! Of course, Mr. Toad felt very ashamed. But the visitor was so pleased with Mr. Toad's garden and the effort he put into making it so nice that the ragged pant leg hanging out of his mouth was overlooked.

"'Fine clothes are not to be compared with fine work,' said the visitor. 'I hereby appoint you as my chief gardener. And so that all may know that this is so, you shall always swallow your old suit whenever you change your clothes!'

"And from that day until now the toads have been the very best gardeners. And in memory of their great, great, great, grandfather they have always swallowed their old suits.

"Now you know what my cousin, old Mr. Toad, did with his old suit just before Peter Rabbit passed by his house this morning," concluded Grandfather Frog.

"Oh," cried the Merry Little Breezes, "thank you for telling us, Grandfather Frog."

Then they raced away across the Green Meadow and up the crooked little path to see if old Mr. Toad was gardening. But Peter Rabbit is still wondering what old Mr. Toad did with his suit, because he didn't mind his own business or notice that Grandfather Frog was hungry, and help him.

DO ALL YOU CAN TO LIVE A PEACEFUL LIFE.
TAKE CARE OF YOUR OWN BUSINESS....
THEN PEOPLE WHO ARE NOT BELIEVERS WILL RESPECT YOU.
I THESSALONIANS 4:11-12

THE VAIN COW

BY ROSEMARY SMITH

Betty was a big, handsome cow. She had velvet-brown eyes, and her coat was as soft as a flower petal. Betty was gentle and kind. She had only one fault. She was very vain.

"How pretty I am!" Betty would exclaim. "What beautiful eyes I have and how smooth my coat is. I am the loveliest cow in the world!"

The other cows sniffed. They laughed at Betty behind her back. Betty and all the cows led a pleasant life. They ate grass and clover. They lay beneath the big trees and watched the clouds make patterns in the sky.

One day Betty wandered away from the other cows. After a while she came to a pool of water. She felt thirsty and bent down to get a drink. There was another cow, looking up at her from the water!

Betty stared at the strange cow for a long time. Then she sighed. This was the loveliest cow she had ever seen!

In the meantime, Rob, the dog, counted the cows and found that Betty was missing. He set out to search for her.

Rob found Betty standing beside the pool. He was all ready to scold her when he saw that she was crying.

"What's wrong?" said Rob.

Betty sighed. "I have found a cow who is more beautiful than I am," she said. Then she showed Rob the cow in the pool of water.

The dog smiled. But he didn't tell Betty that the strange cow was her own reflection in the water. Instead, he gently led her back to the other cows.

Betty said no more about the strange cow. But she never praised her own beauty again. She was quiet and everyone liked her.

DO NOT THINK THAT YOU ARE BETTER THAN YOU ARE.
YOU MUST SEE YOURSELF AS YOU REALLY ARE.
ROMANS 12:3

THE APPLE OF CONTENTMENT

BY HOWARD PYLE

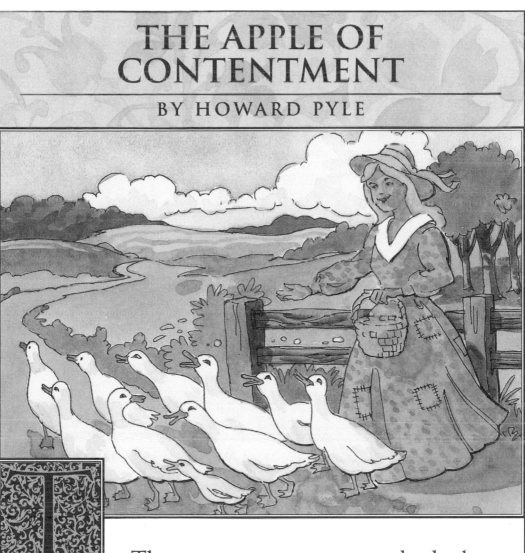

There once was a woman who had three daughters. The first daughter squinted with both eyes, yet the woman loved her as she loved salt, for she also squinted with both eyes. The second daughter had one shoulder higher than the other, and eyebrows as black as charcoal, yet the woman loved her as well as she loved the other, for she also had black eyebrows and one shoulder higher than the other.

The youngest daughter was as pretty as a ripe apple, and had hair as fine as silk and the color of gold, but the woman didn't love her at all, for she herself was neither pretty nor had hair the color of gold.

The first and second sister dressed in their Sunday clothes every day, and sat in the sun doing nothing, just as though they had been born rich ladies. As for Christine, that was the name of the youngest girl, she dressed in nothing but rags and had to take the geese to the hills in the morning and bring them home every night.

The first and second sister had white bread and butter and as much fresh milk as they could drink; but Christine had to eat the rind of the cheese and bread crusts.

One morning Christine started off to the hills with her flock of geese and when she came to the bridge that went over the brook, she saw a little red hat with a bell on the point of it hanging from a bush nearby. It was such a nice pretty little hat that Christine thought she would take it home. So she put it in her pocket, and off she went with her geese to the hills. She had hardly gone a step when she heard a voice calling her, "Christine. Christine."

She looked and all that she saw was a little man with gray hair and a gray beard.

"What do you want?" said Christine. The little man only wanted his hat so that he could go back home in the hills. He had been fishing by the brook on the other side when the wind blew his hat off his head and onto the bush on this side.

"For finding my hat I will give you this seed," said the little man. And he showed her something in his hand that looked like a bean only it was black.

"What kind of seed is that?" asked Christine.

"It is the seed from the apple of contentment. Plant it, and from it will grow a tree, and from the tree will grow an apple. Nobody will be able to pick the apple from the tree but you. And as soon as you pick the apple another will grow in its place."

Christine gave the man his hat and took the seed. That night after bringing the geese back from the hills, she planted it in front of her bedroom window. The next morning when she looked out of the window she saw a beautiful tree. And on the tree hung an apple that shone in the sun as though it were pure gold. She went to the tree and picked that apple.

Being hungry she ate it, and it tasted like pancakes with honey and milk.

Presently the oldest sister came out of the house and looked around, and when she saw the beautiful tree with the golden apple she wanted the apple very badly. She reached and she reached, she climbed and she climbed, but she couldn't get the apple from the tree. At last she had to give up trying.

After a while the second sister came, and when she saw the golden apple she wanted it just as much as the first had. But to want and to get are very different things, as she soon found, for she was no more able to get it than the other sister had been.

Last of all came the mother, and she also tried to pick the apple. But it was no use. She wasn't able to pick the apple either. All that the three could do was to stand under the tree and look at the apple, and wish for it, and wish for it. But as for Christine, if she was hungry or thirsty all she had to do was pick the apple.

One day a king was riding along the road with some of his servants, and saw the apple hanging in the tree. He called on the servant and told him to go and ask whether the apple could be bought. So the servant went up to the house, and knocked on the door.

"What do you want?" asked the mother of the three sisters.

"The king was out riding and saw the golden apple hanging from your tree. Would you sell him the apple for a pot full of gold?" replied the servant.

"Oh, yes!" said the mother, eagerly.

So the servant gave her the pot of gold, and then he tried to pick the apple for the king. First he reached for it, and then he climbed for it, and then he shook the limb of the tree. But it was no use for him to try; he couldn't get it. At last the servant had to go back to the king. The apple was there, he said, and the woman had sold it, but try and try as he might he could not get the apple from the tree.

The king told another servant to go and get the apple for him. But even though this servant was taller and stronger, he couldn't pick the apple from the tree either. So the king decided to go himself to pick the apple. Well, he tried and tried; but he was not able to pick the apple either, and he had to ride away without having even a smell of the apple.

After the king came home, he talked and dreamed and thought of nothing but the apple. He talked to some of his advisors about the tree and how much he wanted the apple. One of his advisors told him that the only one who could pick the apple was the one to whom the tree belonged. When the king heard this he was very glad. He had his horse saddled, and he and his servants rode away. At last they came to the house where Christine lived. There they found the mother and the two older sisters, but Christine was not at home as she was in the hills with the geese.

The king took off his hat and made a fine bow and asked which daughter owned the apple tree.

"Oh, it is my eldest daughter who owns the tree," said the woman. So the king asked the oldest daughter to go pick the apple for him from her tree, and if she would bring it back to him he would marry her and make her his queen.

"Oh, no! That would never do," said the mother. "I can't have my daughter climbing trees in front of the king. If you will go home, she will bring the apple to you."

As soon as the king had left the woman and her daughters went to the hills for Christine. They told her that the king wanted the apple from her tree, and that she must pick it for her sister to take to him. So Christine picked the apple and gave it to her older sister who wrapped it in a napkin and set off to the king's palace. But when she opened the napkin to show the king the apple all that was there was a cold, hard stone.

The king was very upset and told the girl to leave his palace. Then he sent his servant to the house where Christine lived. When the servant arrived at the house, he asked whether the woman had any other daughters.

"Yes, I do. And to tell the truth it is my middle daughter who owns the tree" said the woman. "If you will go home, I will have her pick the apple for the king and bring it to him."

As soon as the servant had gone, they went to the hills to get Christine again so that she could pick another apple for the king. But when the middle daughter took this apple to the King she fared no better than her older sister did. When she opened up her napkin there was nothing there but a lump of mud.

After a while the king's servant came to the house again and asked the woman if she had another daughter.

"Well, yes I do. But she is a poor ragged thing and can only take care of geese," said the woman.

But the servant wanted to see her. So the woman went to the hills to get Christine. When she arrived back at her house, the servant asked Christine if she could pick the apple for the king. Yes, Christine could do that very easily. So she reached and picked it as though it had been nothing but a berry on a bush. Then the servant took off his hat and made her a low bow, for he realized that she was the one whom they were looking for all this time. Christine put the apple in her pocket and went with the servant to the king's palace.

When they arrived everybody began to laugh and point their fingers at Christine for she was just a poor ragged goose girl.

"Have you brought the apple?" asked the king, as soon as Christine had come before him.

"Yes, here it is." Christine took the apple out of her pocket and gave it to the king. Then the king took a great big bite out of it, and as soon as he had done so he looked at Christine and thought that he had never seen such a pretty girl. As for her rags, he didn't think about them anymore than one minds the spots on a cherry. Even though they were married, Christine's mother and sisters didn't mind because they said they still had the apple tree at their house. But the next morning after the wedding the tree stood before the young Queen Christine's window, just

as it had at her old home. That was lucky for the king, for he needed a taste of it now and then as much as anybody else, and no one could pick it for him but Christine.

It is true that serving God makes a person
very rich, if he is satisfied with what he has.
1 Timothy 6:6

A CHILD'S PRAYER

M. BENTHAN-EDWARDS

God make my life a little light,
　Within the world to glow;
A tiny flame that burneth bright
　Wherever I may go.

God make my life a little flow,
　That giveth joy to all,
Content to bloom in native bower,
　Although its place be small.

God make my life a little song,
　That comforteth the sad;
That helpeth others to be strong,
　And makes the singer glad.

God make my life a little staff,
　Whereon the weak may rest,
That so what health and strength I have
　May serve my neighbors best.

JOSIAH: THE BOY KING

2 KINGS 21 23 AND
2 CHRONICLES 33:1-20

After King Manasseh died, his son Amon ruled Judah for about two years. Then Amon's son, Josiah, became King of Judah. He was only eight years old when he became king, but Josiah was the best king Judah had ever had. He always did what God said was right.

When Josiah was sixteen years old, he began to make big changes in Judah. He removed the false gods from Judah and Jerusalem. He destroyed the places for worshiping false gods. He removed the Asherah idols, the wooden and metal idols, and the Baal gods. Then Josiah cut down the incense altars above the idols. He broke up the Asherah idols and the wooden and metal idols. He beat them into powder and sprinkled the powder on the graves of the people who had worshiped those false gods. He burned the bones of their priests on their own altars.

Finally, young King Josiah made the Temple of God in Jerusalem pure again. And he led his people, the people God loved, back to devotion and worship of the one true God of heaven. Josiah was, without a doubt, the greatest king Judah ever had. He was a man like his ancestor, King David, who was the kind of man God wanted.

THERE WAS NO KING LIKE JOSIAH BEFORE OR
AFTER HIM. HE OBEYED THE LORD WITH ALL
HIS HEART, SOUL, AND STRENGTH.
2 KINGS 23:25

THE BOY WHO LOST A DOLLAR

BY ARTHUR MAXWELL

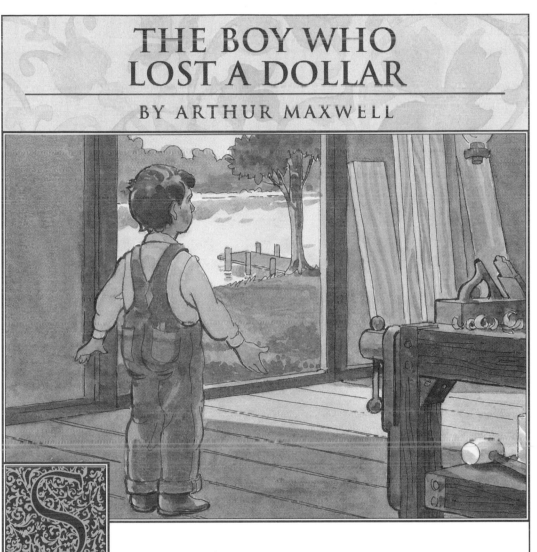

S "Sam," called Father, who was busy hammering in the workshop, "come out here."

"Yes, Dad," mumbled a sleepy voice from indoors.

"Come along, I want you to help me a bit."

"I don't want to come out," said the voice.

"You'd better come out quickly, son. I'm waiting for you."

Sam thought it was about time to move and walked out of the dining room.

"What do you want me to do?" he asked.

"Do?" asked Father. "Why, there's a lot to do. I'm going to build a new chicken shed at the bottom of the garden, and I want you to help carry the lumber down there."

"Umph," growled Sam, "I was just going to start a game...."

"This will be a good game," responded Father. "Come along now and get busy. There's the lumber, and you know where to take it."

"Where do you want me to take it?" asked Sam, trying to delay the work as long as possible.

"Down to the bottom of the garden."

"Which wood do you want me to take?"

"This wood," said Father, starting to get a little upset with Sam.

"But I can't carry all that."

"Yes, you can. Hurry up. I will be down there with the tools before you are down there with the wood."

Sam moved slowly over to the pile of lumber.

"Aw, Dad," he grumbled, "it's too heavy."

"Too heavy! For a big boy like you?"

"I can't lift it," said Sam.

"Why not?"

"It's too heavy."

Sam picked up one plank and let it slip out of his hand with a big crash.

"It's no good," he said, "I can't do it."

"Now look here," said Father, thinking of a good idea, "how soon could you get that wood to the bottom of the garden if I were to give you a dollar?"

"A dollar?" questioned Sam, suddenly forgetting all that he just had been saying. "Would you really give me a dollar for this job?"

"I didn't promise it," replied Father, "but I did ask how long it would take you to carry this to the bottom of the garden if I gave you a dollar."

"I don't know," said Sam, a little uncertain as to what his father was getting at.

"Would you like a dollar for doing this job?" asked Father cheerfully.

"Yes, indeed!" nodded Sam.

"Well," said Father, "before we make the bargain, let me see how fast you could carry it if I did give you a dollar."

"All right," said Sam, seizing the top piece of timber and dashing off down the garden as fast as his legs would go. In less than two minutes he was back again at the shed.

"Was that fast enough?" he asked.

"Yes, that was very good," said Father. "So it wasn't so heavy after all. Now you may go inside and play your game."

"Go inside!" exclaimed Sam, "Why? There's all this wood to carry down to the garden."

"I know," said Father. "That's quite all right. I'll carry it down myself."

"But I want to do it," urged Sam. "I want to earn that dollar you said I could have."

"I am sure you do," said Father, "but it is too late now."

"Too late?" exclaimed Sam. "Why, there is plenty of time before dark."

"Oh, I didn't mean that," said Father, a little sadly. "I mean that if you had done it for me at first, without all that grumbling and growling, I would gladly have given you a dollar and even more for helping me. But if my son will not work for me just for love, I certainly do not want him to do it just for money. I would rather do it all myself."

There was an awkward silence, and Sam walked back to the house to think it over.

Early next morning, as father was shaving in the bathroom, a noise in the back garden caused him to look out of the window. At the bottom of the garden he noticed a strange pile of clean white wood. Halfway up the garden, walking toward the house, was Sam. His face looked as though he was thinking of a big secret.

In a flash Father understood. In another flash he was downstairs, with one side of his face all covered with shaving cream. The next moment he was upstairs in the bathroom again, finishing his interrupted shave. But he had just had time to put something underneath Sam's breakfast plate.

It was the dollar that had been lost and won.

THE REWARDS OF SHOWING LOVE TO OTHERS
ARE OFTEN SURPRISING AND DELIGHTFUL.
SERVE EACH OTHER WITH LOVE.
GALATIANS 5:13

THE LITTLE SNOW MAIDEN

AN IMAGINARY RUSSIAN FOLK TALE

There once was a good man named Peter who lived with his wife, Anna, in a little village on the edge of the forest. Now these two, although they had many friends, were sad because they had no children in their home. Anna never had to run to the door and look out to see that her little child did not wander away, because she had no little child. So Peter and Anna would stand at their window and watch the neighbors' children and wish with all their hearts that they had a child of their own.

One day they saw the children in the sheepskin coats playing in the snow. They made snow forts and threw snowballs at each other, and they laughed and shouted happily. Then they rolled up the snow into a great snow woman and put an old scarf on her head and an old shawl around her shoulders.

"Now, there's an idea," Peter said to Anna. "Let's go out and make a little snow girl. Who knows, maybe she will come alive and be our daughter."

"That is a good idea," said Anna. "It is worth a try."

So the two in their big coats and fur hats went outside. And there in the backyard, where no one could see them, they began to work. They rolled the snow together and began to build it into a little girl.

Well, towards night, when the sky was smoke colored and the clouds were purple, the little snow girl was finished.

"Oh, my little snow girl, speak to us," said Peter.

"Yes, speak to us," said Anna, "and run and skip and laugh like the other children."

Suddenly, in the twilight glow, the little girl's eyelids began to quiver; a faint flush bloomed on her cheeks; her lips parted in a smile. Then her eyes opened, and they were as blue as the sky at noon! All at once, she skipped from her place and began dancing about in the snow and laughing softly, dancing like snowflakes whirled in the wind.

"God be thanked," said Peter. "Now we have a little girl to live with us. Run, Anna, and get a blanket to keep her warm."

So Anna ran and got a blanket and wrapped it about the little snow girl, and Peter picked her up and carried her into the house.

"You must not keep me too warm," the little snow girl said. So Peter put her gently down on a bench farthest from the stove, and she smiled up at him and blew him a kiss. Then Anna got her a little white fur coat, and Peter went to the neighbor's house and bought her a white fur hat and a pair of little white boots with white fur around the tops. But when she was dressed, the little snow girl cried, "It is too hot here in the house. I must go outside."

"No," said Anna, "it is time I tucked you into a warm bed."

"Oh, no," replied the snow girl, "I am a daughter of the snow. I cannot be tucked up under a blanket. I will play by myself in the yard all night." And out she danced into the cold. Over the gleaming snow she skipped, down the silver path of moonlight. Her clothes glittered like diamonds, and the frost shone about her head like a little crown of stars.

For a long time the man and his good wife watched her. "God be thanked for the little girl that has come to us," they said again and again. Then at last they went to bed, but more than once that night they rose to look out of the window and make sure she had not run away. There she was just as before, dancing about in the moonlight and playing all alone.

In the morning she ran into the cottage with shining eyes.

"This is my breakfast," she cried, and she showed the good woman how to crush up a little piece of ice in a wooden bowl, for that was all she would eat. After breakfast she ran out into the road and joined the other children at play. How she played and how the children loved her. She could run faster than all the rest. Her little white boots shined as she ran, and when she laughed, it was like the ringing of tiny silver bells.

The man and the woman watched her and were very proud.

"She is all our own," said Anna.

"Our little snow girl," said Peter.

When it was time, she came in for her ice meal, but though Anna asked her, "Tonight won't you sleep inside?" the little snow girl answered just as before, "Oh, no, I am a little daughter of the snow."

That is how it went all through the winter. The little snow girl made Peter and Anna very happy. She was forever singing and laughing and dancing, in and out of the house. She was very good, too, and she did everything Anna told her. Only she would never sleep inside. She seemed happiest and most at home when the little snow flakes were dancing about in the air.

But when there began to be signs of spring in the air, when the snow melted and one could run down the paths in the forest, when tiny green shoots peeped up here and there, then the little snow girl seemed to be drooping and longing for something. One day she came to Peter and Anna and said:

"Time has come when I must go
To my friends of Frost and Snow.
Good-bye dear ones here, good-bye.
Back I go across the sky."

Peter and Anna began to cry. They wanted her to stay with them.

"My little girl, you must not go!" cried Peter and Anna. And Peter ran and closed the door while Anna put her arms around the little girl, holding her close beside the stove.

"You shall not leave us," they cried. But even as Anna held her tight, she seemed to melt slowly away. At last there was nothing left but a pool of water by the stove with a little fur hat, a little fur coat, and little white boots in the middle of the water.

Yet it seemed to Anna and Peter as though they could see her as she had been before, singing:

"Time has come when I must go
To my friends of Frost and Snow.
Good-bye dear ones here, good-bye.
Back I go across the sky."

"Oh, stay, stay," they begged, but all at once the door burst open. A cold wind swept into the room. When Peter had pushed the door shut again, the little snow maiden had vanished.

Then Peter and Anna wept and thought they should never see her again. Anna carefully laid away the clothes she had left behind. But one starlit night, when winter had come again, Peter and Anna heard a peal of laughter just outside the window.

"That sounds like our little snow girl!" cried Peter, and off he ran to open the door. Sure enough! Into the room she danced, her eyes as shiny as ever, and she sang:

"By frosty night and frosty day
Your love calls me here to stay,
Here till spring I stay and then
Back to frost and snow again."

So Peter and Anna hugged the little snow girl in their arms. She put on her pretty white clothes again, and went out on the gleaming snow, skipping down the path.

Each spring off she went to the north to play through the summer with her friends on the frozen seas. But every winter, she stayed in Russia with Peter and Anna and they came not to mind her going for they knew she would come again. And they thanked God for the changing seasons that brought her to them every year in winter.

MORAL: HOLD GOD'S BLESSINGS WITH AN OPEN HAND
AND THEY WILL KEEP COMING BACK TO YOU.

THE PIED PIPER OF HAMELIN TOWN

ADAPTED FROM THE POEM
BY ROBERT BROWNING

Once a long, long time ago, in
Germany in a region called Brunswick, there
was a pleasant little town known as Hamelin.
It was, in fact, quite pleasant in every single
aspect—save one: Hamelin, you see, was
dreadfully plagued with rats! The houses were

full of them; they were everywhere.

> *Rats!*
> *They fought the dogs and killed the cats,*
> *And bit the babies in the cradles,*
> *And ate the cheeses out of the vats,*
> *And licked the soup from the cooks' own ladles,*
> *Split open the kegs of salted sprats,*
> *Made nests inside men's Sunday hats,*
> *And even spoiled the women's chats*
> *By drowning their speaking*
> *With shrieking and squeaking*
> *In fifty different sharps and flats!*

At last it got so bad that the people simply couldn't stand it any longer, and so they all gathered at the town hall and demanded that the Mayor and the city council of Hamelin put an end to these rats at once. "See here," the outraged citizens cried, "what do we pay your salaries for, anyway? What good are you if you can't do a little thing like rid us of these rats? You had better think of something soon!" they threatened.

> *"Rouse up, sirs! Give your brain a racking*
> *To find the remedy we're lacking,*
> *Or, sure as fate, we'll send you packing!"*

Well, the poor Mayor was in a terrible way, for he could think of no solution whatever. Indeed, he wished that he had never been made Mayor in the first place. He sat in his office with his head in his hands, and he thought, and thought, and thought.

Suddenly there came a little tap-tap at his door. Oh, how the Mayor jumped! His poor heart went racing pit-a-pat at anything like the sound of a rat. But this was just the scraping of some shoes on the mat. And so, relieved, the Mayor said, "Come in!"

And in came the strangest figure!

> *His queer long coat from heel to head*
> *Was half of yellow and half of red,*
> *And he himself was tall and thin,*
> *With sharp blue eyes, each like a pin,*
> *And light loose hair, yet swarthy skin,*
> *No tuft on cheek, no beard on chin,*
> *But lips where smiles went out and in;*
> *There was no guessing his kith and kin:*
> *And nobody could enough admire*
> *The tall man and his quaint attire.*

He really was the strangest fellow! And round his neck he had a long red and yellow ribbon, and on it was hung a flute, or something like a flute anyway, and his fingers went straying up and down it as if he wanted to be playing.

He approached the Mayor and said, "I hear you are troubled with rats in this town."

"I should say we are," groaned the Mayor.

"If you'd like to get rid of them," said the stranger, "I can do it for you."

"You can?" cried the Mayor. "How? Who are you, anyway?"

"I am known as the Pied Piper," said the man, "and I have a way to draw after me everything that walks or flies or swims. Will you give me a thousand guilders if I rid your town of rats?"

"A thousand?" exclaimed the Mayor. "Why, it would be worth fifty thousand guilders to me if you could do what you say. But I don't believe you can."

"All right," said the Piper, "it is a bargain."

And then he went to the door and stepped out into the street and stood; and he put his musical pipe to his lips and began to play a strange, high, little tune.

> And ere three shrill notes the pipe uttered,
> You heard as if any army muttered;
> And the muttering grew to a grumbling;
> And the grumbling grew to a mighty rumbling;
> And out of the houses the rats came tumbling!
> Great rats, small rats, lean rats, brawny rats,
> Brown rats, black rats, gray rats, tawny rats,
> Grave old plodders, gay young friskers,
> Fathers, mothers, uncles, cousins,
> Cocking tails and pricking whiskers,
> Families by tens and dozens,
> Brothers, sisters, husbands, wives—
> Followed the Piper for their lives!

From street to street he piped, advancing, from street to street they followed, dancing. Up one street and down another, till they came right down to the edge of the big river, and there the Piper turned sharply about and stepped aside, and all those rats tumbled hurry-scurry, head over heels, down the bank into the river and—were—drowned. Every single last rat, except one big old fat rat, who managed to swim across the river and carry the story of what happened back home to Rat Land.

Well, the town erupted with joy, now that it was finally rid of all the dreaded rats. The people, old and young alike, waved their hats and jumped up and down with glee.

> *You should have heard the Hamelin people*
> *Ringing the bells till they rocked the steeple.*
> *"Go," cried the Mayor, "and get long poles,*
> *Poke out the nests and block up the holes!*
> *Consult with carpenters and builders,*
> *And leave in our town not even a trace*
> *Of the rats!"—when suddenly, up the face*
> *Of the Piper perked in the marketplace,*
> *With a, "First, if you please, my thousand guilders!"*

"H'm—er—a thousand guilders—well," said the Mayor. "Oh, you mean that little joke I made a while ago. Of course that was all a joke, don't you see?"

"I do not joke," said the Piper in a quiet but stern manner. "So I'll have my thousand guilders now, if you please."

"Oh, come now," said the Mayor, "you know very well that it isn't worth a single guilder to play a simple tune like that.

But, just to show you how generous we are, here, take fifty and be done with it."

"A bargain is a bargain," said the Piper. "For the last time—will you give me my thousand guilders?"

"I'll give you a pipe of tobacco, something good to eat, and call you lucky at that!" snapped the Mayor, tossing his head back.

Then the Piper's mouth grew strange and thin, and sharp blue and green lights began dancing in his eyes, and he said to the Mayor very softly, "I know another tune than that which I played; I play it to those who play me false."

"Play what you please!" replied the Mayor. "You can't frighten me! Go ahead, do your worst!"

Once more the Piper stepped into the street, put the pipe to his lips, and began to play a little tune. It was quite a different little tune this time, soft and sweet and very, very strange. And before he played three little notes,

> *There was a rustling that seemed like a bustling*
> *Of merry crowds justling at pitching and hustling;*
> *Small feet were pattering, wooden shoes clattering,*
> *And, like fowls in a farmyard when barley is scattering,*
> *Out came the children running,*
> *All the little boys and girls,*

With rosy cheeks and flaxen curls,
And sparkling eyes and teeth like pearls,
Tripping and skipping, ran merrily after
The wonderful music with shouting and laughter.

"Stop, stop!" cried the people. "He is taking our children! Stop him, Mayor!"

"I will give you your money; I promise I will!" cried the Mayor, and he tried to run after the Piper.

But the very same music that made the children dance made the grown-up people stand stock-still; it was as if their feet had been tied to the ground; they could not move a muscle. There they stood and saw the Piper move slowly down the street, playing his little tune, with the children dancing at his heels.

On and on he went, on and on the children danced, till he came to the bank of the river.

"Oh, no!" the people cried, "he's going to drown our children in the river!" But the Piper turned and went along by the riverbank, and all the children followed after. Up, and up, and up the hill they went, straight toward the mountain that overlooks the city. When suddenly, the mountainside opened—just like two great doors, and the Piper went through the opening, still playing the little tune, and the children danced after him—and—just as they got through—the great doors slid together again and shut them all in! Every last one of them, except one little lame child, who couldn't keep up with the rest and didn't get there in time. And the children were never seen again, never.

But years and years afterwards, when the fat old rat who swam across the river was a grandfather, his children would ask him, "What made you follow the music, Grandfather?" and he would tell them, "My dears, when I heard that tune, I thought I heard the moving aside of pickle-crate covers, and the leaving ajar of pantry doors, and I smelled the most delicious old cheese in the world, and I saw sugar barrels ahead of me; and then, just as a great yellow cheese seemed to be saying, 'Come on, bore into me'—I felt the river rolling over me!"

And, in the same way, the people asked the little lame child, "What made you follow the music?"

"I do not know what the others heard," he said, "but I, when the Piper began to play, I heard a voice that told of a wonderful country just ahead, where the bees had no stings, and the horses had wings, and the trees bore wonderful fruits, where no one was tired or lame, and children played all day; and just as the beautiful country was one step away—the mountain closed on my playmates, and I was left alone."

That was all the people ever knew. The children never came back. All that was left of the Piper and the rats was just the big street that led to the river, which they renamed Pied Piper Street, and a town full of people who had learned never to go back on a promise.

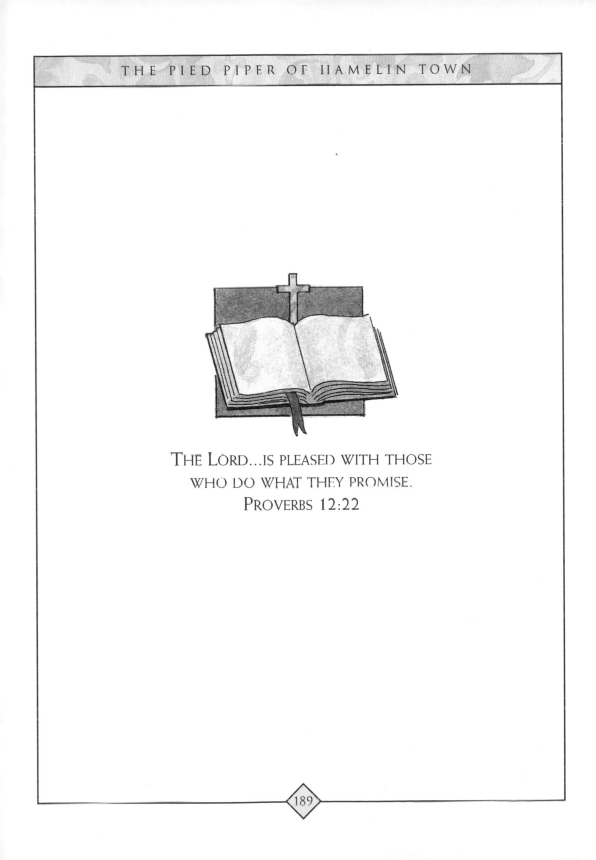

THE LORD...IS PLEASED WITH THOSE
WHO DO WHAT THEY PROMISE.
PROVERBS 12:22

ALL THINGS BEAUTIFUL

CECIL FRANCES ALEXANDER

All things bright and beautiful,
All creatures great and small,
All things wise and wonderful,
The Lord God made them all.

Each little flower that opens,
Each little bird that sings,
He made their glowing colors,
He made their tiny wings.

The purple-headed mountain,
The river running by,
The sunset, and the morning,
That brighten up the sky;

The cold wind in the winter,
The pleasant summer sun,
The ripe fruits in the garden,
He made them every one.

The tall trees in the greenwood,
The meadows where we play,
The rushes by the water,
We gather every day;

He gave us eyes to see them,
And lips that we might tell
How great is God Almighty,
Who has made all things well.

COLIN COLLIE

ROSEMARY SMITH

Colin Collie was an only child. Everyone in the neighborhood agreed that he was spoiled.

"That Colin," Mrs. Airedale complained, "is noisy and rude."

"It's all his mother's fault," answered Mrs.

Scotty. "She lets the child do anything he wants."

Mrs. Collie once had four little puppies. But three of them had died and only Colin was left. His mother loved him so much that she could never say no to him.

None of the other puppies in the neighborhood would play with Colin. "He always wants everything his way," said Jimmy Great Dane. Colin was lonesome and unhappy.

One day the little collie was sitting in the lane. Suddenly, he heard a loud "peep, peep!" Two chicks ran past him. A kitten was chasing them.

Colin caught hold of the kitten and scolded her. "You mustn't hurt those poor chicks," he said.

"But I'm so hungry," mewed the kitten.

"Haven't you got any mother or home?" asked Colin.

"No," answered the kitten, "I have to find my own food."

Colin felt sorry for the kitten. She looked thin and tired. He decided to take her home with him.

Mrs. Collie was surprised when she saw the kitten. "We haven't much for dinner," she whispered.

"That's all right," said Colin. "The kitten can have my share."

The kitten moved in with Mrs. Collie and Colin. She was soon plump and healthy again. Colin and the kitten played together.

Soon, the other youngsters in the neighborhood started playing with Colin and the kitten. They found that Colin was no longer selfish.

WHEN YOU DO THINGS, DO NOT LET SELFISHNESS
OR PRIDE BE YOUR GUIDE.... DO NOT BE INTERESTED
ONLY IN YOUR OWN LIFE, BUT BE INTERESTED
IN THE LIVES OF OTHERS.
PHILIPPIANS 2:3-4

THE GIFT OF THE MAGI

BY O. HENRY

One dollar and eighty-seven cents. That was all. And sixty cents of it was in pennies saved one and two at a time. Three times Della counted it. One dollar and eighty-seven cents. And the next day would be Christmas.

There was clearly nothing to do but flop down on the shabby little couch and cry. So Della did, which shows that life is made up of sobs, sniffles, and smiles.

In the hall below was a mailbox into which no letter would go and an electric doorbell from which no finger could coax a ring. Also on the mailbox was a card bearing the name "Mr. James Dillingham Young." The "Dillingham" had been added during a former period of prosperity when its possessor was being paid thirty dollars per week. Now, when the income was shrunk to twenty dollars, though, they were thinking seriously of changing it to a modest and unassuming D. But whenever Mr. James Dillingham Young came home and reached his flat above, he was called "Jim." And greatly hugged by Mrs. James Dillingham Young, already introduced to you as Della, which is all very good.

Della finished her cry and put powder on her cheeks. She stood by the window and looked out at a gray cat walking along a gray fence in a gray backyard. Tomorrow would be Christmas Day, and she had only a dollar and eighty-seven cents with which to buy Jim a present. She had been saving every penny she could for months, with this result. Twenty dollars a week doesn't go far. Expenses had been greater than she had calculated. They always are. Only a dollar and eighty-seven cents to buy a present for Jim. Her Jim. Many a happy hour she had spent planning for something nice for him.

Something fine and rare and sterling—something just a little bit worthy of the honor of being owned by Jim. There was a pier-glass between the windows of the room. Perhaps you have seen a pier-glass in an eight dollar flat. A very thin and very agile person may, by looking at his reflection in a rapid sequence of long strips, get a fairly accurate idea of his looks. Della, being slender, had mastered the art. Suddenly she whirled from the window and stood before the glass. Her eyes were shining brilliantly, but her face had lost its color within twenty seconds. Rapidly she pulled down her hair and let it fall to its full length. Now, there were two possessions of the James Dillingham Young's in which they both took a mighty pride. One was Jim's gold watch that had been his father's and his grandfather's. The other was Della's hair. Had the Queen of Sheba lived in the flat across the hall, Della would have let her hair hang out the window some day to dry just to outshine Her Majesty's jewels and gifts. Had King Solomon been the janitor, with all his treasures piled up in the basement, Jim would have pulled out his watch every time he passed, just to see the king pluck at his beard from envy.

So now Della's beautiful hair fell about her rippling and shining like a cascade of brown waters. It reached below her knees and made itself almost a garment for her. And then she did it up again nervously and quickly. Once she faltered for a minute and stood still while a tear or two splashed on the worn red carpet. On went her old brown jacket; on went her old brown hat. With a whirl of skirts and with the brilliant sparkle still in her eyes, she fluttered out the door and down the stairs to the street. Where she stopped the sign read: "Mrs. Sofronie. Hair Goods of All Kinds." One flight up Della ran and collected herself, panting. Madame, large, too white, chilly, hardly looked liked the "Sofronie."

"Will you buy my hair?" asked Della.

"I buy hair," said Madame. "Take your hat off, and let's have a look it." Down rippled the brown cascade.

"Twenty dollars," said Madame, lifting the mass with a practiced hand.

"Give it to me quickly," said Della.

Oh, and the next two hours flew by on rosy wings.

She was ransacking the stores for Jim's present. She found it at last. It surely had been made for Jim and no one else. There was no other like it in any of the stores, and she had turned all of them inside out. It was a platinum fob chain, simple and chaste in design, properly proclaiming its value by substance alone and not by silly decoration—as all good things should do. It was even worthy of The Watch. As soon as she saw it she knew that it must be Jim's. It was like him. Quietness and value—the description applied to both. Twenty-one dollars they took from her for it, and she hurried home with the eighty-seven cents. With that chain on his watch, Jim might be properly anxious about the time in any company. Grand as the watch was, he sometimes looked at it on the sly because of the old leather strap that he used in place of a chain.

When Della reached home her excitement gave way a little to wisdom and reason. She got out her curling iron and went to work repairing the ravages to her hair made by generosity added to love. And that is always a tremendous task, dear friends—a mammoth task. Within forty minutes her head was covered with tiny, close-lying curls that made her look wonderfully like a truant schoolboy. She looked at her reflection in the mirror long, carefully, and critically.

"If Jim doesn't kill me," she said to herself, "before he takes a second look at me, he'll say I look like a Coney Island chorus girl. But what could I do—oh! what could I do with a dollar and eighty-seven cents?"

At seven o'clock the coffee was made, and the frying-pan was on the back of the stove hot and ready to cook the chops. Jim was never late. Della doubled the fob chain in her hand and sat on the corner of the table near the door that he always entered. Then she heard his step on the stairway down on the first flight, and she turned white for just a moment. She had a habit of saying little silent prayers about the simplest everyday things. Now she whispered, "Please God, make him think I am still pretty."

The door opened and Jim stepped in and closed it. He looked thin and very serious. Poor fellow, he was only twenty-two,—and to be burdened with a family! He needed a new overcoat, and he was without gloves. Jim stopped inside the door, as immovable as a setter at the scent of quail. His eyes were fixed upon Della, and there was an expression in them that she could not read, and it terrified her. It was not anger, nor surprise, nor disapproval, nor horror, nor any of the sentiments for which she had been prepared. He simply stared at her with that peculiar expression on his face. Della wriggled off the table and went for him.

"Jim, darling," she cried, "don't look at me that way. I had my hair cut off and sold because I couldn't have lived through Christmas without giving you a present. It'll grow out again—you won't mind, will you? I just had to do it. My hair grows awfully fast. Say 'Merry Christmas' Jim, and let's be happy. You don't know what a nice—what a beautiful, nice gift I've got for you."

"You've cut off your hair?" asked Jim, slowly, as if he had not arrived at that fact yet, even after the hardest mental labor.

"Cut it off and sold it," said Della. "Don't you like me just as well, anyhow? I'm me without my hair, don't you think?"

Jim looked about the room curiously. "You say your hair is

gone?" he said, with an air almost of idiocy.

"You needn't look for it," said Della. "It's sold, I tell you—sold and gone, too. It's Christmas Eve. Be good to me, for it went for you. Maybe the hairs of my head were numbered," she went on with sudden serious sweetness, "but nobody could ever count my love for you. Shall I put the chops on, Jim?"

Out of his trance Jim seemed quickly to wake. He hugged his Della. Eight dollars a week or a million a year—what is the difference? A genius or a wit would give you the wrong answer. The magi brought valuable gifts, but that was not among them. This dark fact will be shown later on. Jim drew a package from his overcoat pocket and threw it upon the table.

"Don't make any mistake, Dell," he said, "about me. I don't think there's anything in the way of a haircut or a shave or a shampoo that could make me like my girl any less. But if you'll unwrap that package you may see why you had me going a while at first."

White fingers and nimble tore at the string and paper. And then an ecstatic scream of joy. And then, alas! a quick change to tears and wails. For there lay The Combs—the set of combs, side and back, that Della had worshiped long in a Broadway window. Beautiful combs, pure tortoise shell, with jeweled rims—just the shade to wear in the beautiful vanished hair. They were expensive combs, she knew, and her heart had simply craved and yearned over them without the least hope of owning them. And now, they were hers, but the tresses that should have adorned the coveted combs were gone. She hugged them to her bosom, and at length she was able to

look up with dim eyes and a smile and say, "My hair grows so fast, Jim!"

And then Della leaped up like a little singed cat and cried, "Oh, oh!"

Jim had not yet seen his beautiful present. She held it out to him eagerly upon her open palm. The dull precious metal seemed to flash with a reflection of her bright and ardent spirit.

"Isn't it a dandy, Jim? I hunted all over town to find it. You'll have to look at the time a hundred times a day now. Give me your watch. I want to see how it looks on it."

Instead of obeying, Jim tumbled down on the couch and put his hands under the back of his head and smiled.

"Dell," said he, "let's put our Christmas presents away and keep them a while. They're too nice to use just at present. I sold the watch to get the money to buy your combs. And now suppose you put the chops on."

The magi, as you know, were wise men—wonderfully wise men—who brought gifts to the Baby Jesus in the manger. They invented the art of giving Christmas presents. Being wise, their gifts were no doubt wise ones that could be exchanged in case of duplication. And here I have lamely told you the story of two foolish people in an apartment who most unwisely sacrificed for each other the greatest treasures of their house.

But in a last word to the wise of today let it be said that, of all who give gifts these two people were the wisest. They gave the very best they had to the one they loved. Of all who give and receive gifts, people like these are wisest. Everywhere they are wisest. They are the magi.

MORAL: THE REWARD OF GIVING UP SOMETHING DEAR FOR SOMEONE YOU LOVE IS GREATER THAN THE SACRIFICE.

AUTHOR INDEX

ACKNOWLEDGMENTS

Reasonable care has been taken to trace ownership and,
when necessary, obtain permission for each selection.

Beard, Patten. "The Little White Bed That Ran Away." From *Tucked-in Tales.*
Chicago: Rand McNally and Company, 1941.

Browning, Robert "The Pied Piper of Hamelin Town." From *More Classics
to Read Aloud to Your Children*, edited by William F. Russell, Ed.D. New
York: Crown Publishers, Inc., copyright ©1986 by William F. Russell.
Used by permission.

Burgess, Gelett. "The Steamboat and the Locomotive." From *Through The
Gate of My Book House*, edited by Olive Beaupré Miller. Chicago: The
Book House for Children, 1920, 1925, 1928, 1937.

Burgess, Thorton W. "Mr. Toad's Old Suit," *Grandfather Frog and Friends.*
New York: John H. Eggers Co., Inc., 1922.

Fitzhugh, Percy K. "Changeable Arthur," *Golden Rod Storybook.* New York:
McLoughlin Bros. Publishers, 1906.

Harrison, Elizabeth. "A Man With a Dream." From *Up One Pair of Stairs of
My Book House*. Chicago: The Book House for Children, 1920, 1925,
1928, 1937.

Kohler, Julilly House. "The Little Boy Who Wasn't Lost." *Story Parade
Magazine*, August 1949.

Larcom, Lucy. "How Margery Wondered." From *McGuffey's Fourth Eclectic
Reader*. New York: American Book Company, 1879.

Lofting, Hugh. "Puddleby," *The Story of Dr. Dolittle*. Frederick A. Stokes
Co., 1920.

"The Little Snow Maiden: A Russian Folk Tale." From *Up One Pair of Stairs of My Book House*. Chicago: The Book House for Children, 1920, 1925, 1928, 1937.

Maxwell, Arthur S. "Nellie's Wish," "The Boy Who Lost a Dollar," and "Smiles," *Uncle Arthur's Bedtime Stories*. Washington, DC: Review and Herald Publishing Association, 1927, 1941.

Pyle, Howard. "The Apple of Contentment." From *Pepper and Salt*. Harper and Brothers, 1885, 1913.

Smith, Rosemary. "The Calf and the Colt," "The Vain Cow," and "Colin Collie," *The Big Book of Animal Stories*. Kenosha, WI: John Martin's House, Inc., 1944.